Popular Amphibians

FROM THE EXPERTS AT
ADVANCED VIVARIUM SYSTEMS™

Philippe de Vosjoli

THE HERPETOCULTURAL LIBRARY™
Advanced Vivarium Systems™
Irvine, California

Karla Austin, *business operations manager*
Jarad Krywicki, *editor*
Erin Kuechenmeister, *production editor*
Nick Clemente, *special consultant*
Designed by Michael Vincent Capozzi
All photos by Philippe de Vosjoli
Rachel Rice, *indexer*

Cover photography by Mark Kostich

LCCN: 96-183295
ISBN:1-882770-60-9

An Imprint of BowTie Press®
A Division of BowTie, Inc.
3 Burroughs
Irvine, CA 92618
www.avsbooks.com
(877) 4-AVS-BOOK

We want to hear from you. What books would you like to see in the future? Please feel free to write us with any comments on our AVS books.

Printed in Singapore
10 9 8 7 6 5 4 3 2 1

CONTENTS

ACKNOWLEDGMENTS

S pecial thanks go to the following friends for their support, advice, and guidance in the course of assembling the material for this book: Ed and Liddy Kammer of West Coast Reptiles provided animals, direction, information about imports, and interesting late-night discussions on the future of herpetoculture. Chris Estep at Reptile Haven supported the project by offering supplies along with good company, humor, sarcasm, and valuable comments. Ray Busby and David Masur of International Reptile Breeders Association (IRBA) deserve special recognition for supporting my obsession with naturalistic vivaria. Through their San Diego IRBA Vivarium show held in October, they were the first to provide a recognized outlet for vivarium design artists and set a trend that is now spreading nationwide. Credit for inspiration for the chapter about the use of vivaria in education goes to Dan McCarron, a teacher with a vision. Last but not least, I am indebted to Susan Donoghue, V.M.D., for ongoing cutting-edge dialogue and her review of the manuscript.

INTRODUCTION

A lthough I've kept amphibians for decades, I still can't help watching common species in pet shops and herp (amphibians and reptiles) shows. These fascinating animals come in a variety of sizes, shapes, colors, and personalities, but all seem designed to enchant their owners. Nocturnal species appeal to night owls, while brightly colored, active species make superb daily attractions in naturalistic vivaria (enclosures for live animals). Amphibians excel as children's pets, centerpieces in planted vivaria, research subjects for amateur biologists, and a lifelong passion for serious herpetoculturists.

For all their beauty and charm, amphibians are relatively fragile animals that require specific temperatures, foods, and enclosures. The species discussed in this book require water or high humidity to thrive, and keepers must pay special attention to the quality of their water. Keeping a pet amphibian healthy and happy requires knowledge about its needs. In this book, I give step-by-step details about amphibian care. You'll learn how best to keep your new pet and how to help it thrive for years to come.

In recent years, the popularity of frogs and salamanders as pets has surged. To keep up with the demand, several species are collected from the wild by the thousands and are now standard fare in pet stores. Unfortunately, these mass-collected species tend to be inexpensive and sold as disposable living toys, typically marketed to appeal to children rather than adults. Because these amphibians are most often marketed to children, the habitats recommended for keeping them are sadly unsophisticated. Consumers often see these amazing creatures in austere and Spartan environments—small, unlit, plastic terrariums without plants or filters. These special and beautiful creatures end up debased by the setting in which they appear. This inhumane approach creates far-ranging negative consequences, and it performs a great disservice to the animals (which live impoverished lives and die prematurely) *and* to the children and adults who purchase them.

In contrast, amphibians kept in attractive, enriched environments display a greater range of behaviors and far longer life spans, providing years of beautiful and captivating activities. These biologically complex (but easy to make) naturalistic vivaria encourage study, creativity, research, and an evolving awareness of the natural world.

Taking the above ideas into consideration, this book plans to present the correct way to keep frogs, newts, and salamanders, with an emphasis on the step-by-step design of decorative and functional vivaria. To the surprise of many, these setups are relatively easy to maintain and comparatively inexpensive, costing about the same as basic aquarium systems for tropical fish. Indeed, many of the species covered in this book can be successfully kept with fish.

This book also aims to raise consciousness and promote education. To address these issues, I included chapters about the benefits of vivaria in the work place and the use of amphibians in naturalistic vivaria as a valuable tool for teaching biology.

As long as I've kept amphibians and as much as I love to watch the frogs and salamanders in pet shops, I'm also aware of the important issues facing wild populations of these creatures. Unmonitored and unmanaged exploitation of amphibians is not acceptable. If we are to continue to be able to keep frogs and salamanders in captivity, we must give attention to conservation, sustainable use, management, and commercial herpetoculture of these species.

CHAPTER 1

SELECTION

Before Buying Frogs and Newts

Frogs and newts are beautiful, fascinating creatures that can enrich your life. However, they must be researched and examined before purchase, not purchased on a whim. Many require specific conditions, such as cool temperatures and live foods, and the design of their setups requires thought and planning. As a rule, frogs and newts are relatively inexpensive, although their setups, if done right, end up costing between sixty and one hundred dollars.

The Oriental fire-bellied toad *(Bombina orientalis)* is one of the gems of the frog world. Fortunately, it is readily available and easy to keep and breed.

At the outset, ask yourself whether a frog or newt is the right pet for you. What is it that you expect from owning a frog or newt? They are not particularly responsive personal pets and they can't be handled, so any pleasure you derive from them will be from observation. Only close scrutiny reveals the special beauty of these creatures, their unusual forms, their golden eyes, their porcelain skin, the details of their skin texture and pattern, and their variety of colors—from subtle to vivid hues. Interesting patterns and behaviors add to the charm of these little beings, which fascinate their owners precisely because they are so alien. Once you realize that observing these animals provides enjoyment, the importance of designing an attractive natural-looking display—a living work of art—becomes obvious.

Selecting Species
The best way to select a species is to refer to books with photographs or, better yet, go to a store and observe live animals. Once you have found a species that appeals to you, take the time to read about its natural history, captive care, and requirements for designing a proper setup, which you'll find in this book.

Southeast Asian green-back frogs *(Rana ery-thraea)* are very beautiful ranids, not as rapacious as leopard frogs, and generally very amenable to keeping in vivaria.

Beware of Heat!
Many temperate amphibian species, particularly salamanders, fare well during cool months but have high mortality rates on hot summer days. Various salamanders and frogs, such as fire-bellied newts and Oriental fire-bellied toads, end up dying when temperatures rise above 80° Fahrenheit (F) and head toward 85° F. Many deaths occur during summer heat waves. If you live in a warm area, select amphibians more adapted to warm temperatures, which excludes the great majority of salamanders.

Next, plan your vivarium, including the size, type, and supplies needed to assemble it. Only after having completed the vivarium should you purchase or collect the species you intend to keep. If you plan to collect a species in the wild, make sure you follow the conservation guidelines and laws in your area. Wild-caught specimens are, in general, far less hardy than captive-bred animals.

Another way to decide what species to keep is to first decide on the type of display you want. Many hobbyists are more interested in creating a type of display, either an aquarium or a shoreline vivarium, with frogs and newts as one of the aesthetic components of the setup. To help in your selection, refer to the following categories that match setups and amphibians. The groupings do not imply compatibility of species.

Amphibians suitable for **aquaria** and **deep island aquaria** (more than half-filled):

❏ clawed frog

❏ dwarf clawed frog

❏ axolotl

❏ certain newts

❏ tadpoles

Amphibians suitable for **island aquaria** (half-filled):

❏ dwarf clawed frog

❏ floating frog

❏ fire-bellied toad

❏ newts

Species suitable for **shoreline vivaria:**

❏ floating frog

❏ fire-bellied toad

❏ leopard frog

❏ newts

❏ salamanders

The type of food required by frogs, newts, or other salamanders might affect your species selection. Most frogs and salamanders, with the exception of some aquatic species, require live, moving prey, which usually means a weekly visit to the pet store to buy crickets, black worms, or other live foods. Fire-bellied toads, floating frogs, leopard frogs, and salamanders need live foods two to three times a week. If routine purchase of live food is a problem, consider aquatic species that eat frozen foods or commercial diets. These include dwarf underwater frogs, clawed frogs, axolotls, and newts.

Newts, such as this Chinese paddle-tailed newt *(Pachytriton labiatum)*, are often presented in the worst possible manner in pet stores. Kept the right way they easily rival tropical fish as aquarium displays.

CHAPTER 2

QUARANTINE AND ACCLIMATION

Regrettably, most species covered in this book are collected from the wild, transported, held in overcrowded conditions, and starved for varying periods of time before landing in the local pet store. These conditions make it highly probable that the animals you buy will be thin, stressed, and hosts to parasites or bacterial and viral pathogens.

Although your new frog or newt might appear healthy, it might be in a disease-incubation stage, soon to be overcome by pathogens. Indeed, newly imported amphibians often initially seem in good health only to have a sudden crash or decline within the first week or two after purchase (see "Crash Syndrome" in Diseases and Disorders).

Because of the risk of spreading disease, experienced keepers always quarantine new animals (keeping them separate until they have proven healthy) before introducing them into a setup with established animals. Many established animals have been wiped out because of the introduction of new animals without quarantine. However, if the animals you purchase come from the same tank and are the only ones you plan to keep, quarantine is not necessary.

During quarantine, which should be a minimum of thirty days, monitor the health of your animals. Keep track of their attitude, alertness, and feeding activity, the condition of their feces, their ability to gain and maintain weight, and their behavior. Inactivity, hyperactivity, spastic behaviors, failure to feed, watery feces, weight loss, discolored skin patches, and cloudy eyes are all signs of possible disease.

Most of the amphibians covered in this book can be quarantined in 10-gallon tanks with screen tops. In general, aquatic species fare well in bare tanks with a sponge filter, a few potted aquatic plants, and an underwater shelter. For semiaquatic species, such as newts or floating frogs, use partially filled tanks with islands made of inverted flower pots with a piece of cork and strands of elodea *(Egeria densa)* as temporary housing. Keep land dwellers such as tiger salamanders on moistened green moss and provide them with a shelter and a shallow water container. Read the chapter about housing for further details.

In this quarantine setup for most newts, a Foam Home polyurethane foam background provides surface areas and hollows that make the newts feel more secure. A section of cork was wedged between the foam and front glass to allow access to land.

Inexpensive utility sinks are invaluable for quarantining groups of newts or frogs. A screen cover is required for frogs and recommended with newts and salamanders to prevent escape.

A quarantine setup for semiaquatic frogs should have a low level of water, and cork bark or foam platforms. Place white paper under the tank to monitor the state of the feces. If a large foam platform and cork bark shelters are used, this system will also work well for various salamanders. Make sure you have a secure lid.

The substrate of this simple setup for quarantine of terrestrial and semiaquatic salamanders is a gravel bed covered with moist green moss. Cork bark shelters are placed on the moss and a shallow and easily accessible water container is sunk into the gravel. This kind of setup can also be used with semiterrestrial and terrestrial frogs, such as leopard frogs, rice paddy frogs, and even fire-bellied toads. The moss must be kept moist.

Non-release Practices

Never release unwanted or sick animals into the wild. It is illegal. Moreover, most released amphibians do not survive. In addition, there is a chance that you could threaten native wildlife by exposing them to foreign pathogens. Unwanted pets should always be sold or given to pet businesses, other hobbyists, or animal shelters—never released. Unwanted sick amphibians are best euthanized.

CHAPTER 3

HOUSING

Enclosures

The best enclosures for keeping amphibians are all-glass tanks with sliding screen tops or aquaria with screen tops. Open-top aquaria work for some aquatic species, such as dwarf underwater frogs and axolotls, as long as the water level remains at least a couple of inches below the top of the tank. Floating frogs can be housed safely with dwarf clawed frogs in half-filled tanks.

The plastic terrariums commonly recommended for keeping frogs and newts can be used as temporary housing and for quarantining smaller amphibians, but they are unsuitable as display enclosures. Plastic terrariums become easily scratched and unsanitary, and they have no visual appeal. When keeping frogs and newts, the saying "glass has class" holds true.

This display by Reptile Haven (Oceanside, CA) won first prize in the aquatic division at the 2000 IRBA Vivarium show in San Diego. It housed several paddle-tailed newts. The background was a polyurethane Foam Home unit. In the center, a weighted cork round was planted with *cryptocorynes*. Java fern and anubias were anchored to the foam background. A powerhead in the foam unit acted as a filter and current generator.

If you have limited space, such as a desktop, start with a tank as small as 2 gallons for tiny species such as dwarf clawed frogs, floating frogs, or Oriental fire-bellied newts. For the other species covered in this book, you'll need at least a 10-gallon tank, though larger tanks—20 gallons or more—are preferred. In larger tanks, the quality of water and substrate (bottom material) remains more stable and requires less maintenance. The animals also utilize the extra space.

The importance of screen tops for most amphibians cannot be emphasized enough. Thousands of captive frogs and newts end up as mummified dust balls because their owners failed to provide an aquarium cover. Most newts, salamanders, toads, and frogs can escape an uncovered tank—and once they do, they will not survive.

Shallow Shoreline Vivarium

For semiaquatic species, such as Oriental fire-bellied toads and newts, gravel bed shoreline vivaria might be the easiest setups to design and maintain. As the name indicates, this type of vivarium includes a substrate of gravel that simulates the shoreline of a stream or pond, combining equal areas of shallow water and land. To create this kind of setup, first pour a 1- to 2 ½-inch layer of a washed ¼- to ½-inch diameter aquarium gravel or fired clay substrate used for growing aquatic plants. The next step is to shift part of the substrate to one side and create a depression. This area will become the water section. For most species, this depression should cover ⅓ to ½ of the floor surface, depending on the habits of the animals you plan to introduce (less for primarily ground-dwelling species, more for primarily aquatic ones). The depression should be 3 to 4 inches deep. Landscape the land/gravel area with rocks, wood, and plants. Add small sections of wood and smooth pebbles along the water's edges to give the vivarium character and to hold the gravel in place. Leave open areas for easy access to and from the land area.

Select plants that grow well hydroponically (in water), such as Chinese evergreen (*Aglaonema* sp.), pothos, arrowhead plants (*Sagittaria* spp.), and variegated Wandering Jew *(Zebrina pendula)*. These can be planted in the gravel land sections. Simply remove plants from their pots, wash their roots free of soil, and insert them into the gravel layer. Then add cork bark sections to the land area to provide shelters and dry platforms. Cover the exposed gravel on the land with moistened green moss. Add water to the gravel depression, to a level about two-thirds the height of the land section.

One or two bulbs in a fluorescent fixture running the length of the tank provide the necessary light. For species that like to bask, such as fire-bellied toads or leopard frogs, place an additional low-wattage bulb in a small reflector-type fixture over a basking site, such as sections of wood, rock, or an open gravel area.

This shallow shoreline vivarium was designed to include treefrogs and anoles.

Gravel bed vivaria are easy to set up and can be very decorative. In this setup, round pebbles line the edge of the water section.

Weekly Water Changes

The water in a shoreline vivarium should be changed weekly. In small setups, use a turkey baster to remove the water. With deeper water, use a siphon or, even better, a manual sump pump. Before siphoning or pumping old water, pour additional water over the land area to lightly flush the gravel surface and to drive waste into the water section. When replacing the water, pour new water into the water section, not the land area, so that it is relatively clean and free of debris.

The water in this shoreline tank is being drained with a manual boat bilge pump. You can also use siphons and industrial vacuum cleaners for this purpose. Whatever you do, never start a siphon using your mouth.

Flushing

At least once a month, flush the gravel bed more thoroughly. To do this, pour greater amounts of water over the land area and siphon out the flushed water from the water section. Two to three flushes will clear out a significant amount of waste while retaining enough bacterial colonization in the gravel to still act as a biological filter.

This is a basic inexpensive shoreline setup. The land area is a gravel bed. The plants are Chinese evergreen rinsed free of soil and planted in the gravel. A layer of moist moss covers most of the land area. A section of cork serves as a shelter. A low-wattage incandescent bulb over a basking site or a fluorescent bulb is used for lighting. The water can be changed using a small plastic container or a turkey baster.

Advanced Shoreline Vivaria

You can create a larger, more complex shoreline vivaria (at least 6 square feet) by planting a variety of shoreline plants and increasing the lighting over parts of the water section.

Along the shoreline, add Java moss *(Vesicularia dubyana)* into the water. With time, the moss will creep partially onto wood, cork, and rough rock while spreading in the water section. Also place semiaquatic plants, such as dwarf umbrella *(Cyperus alternifolius* dwarf), sweet flag *(Acorus gramineus)*, slender arrowhead *(Sagittaria graminea)*, *Anubias* spp., sword plants *(Echinodorus* spp.), and pennywort *(Hydrocotyle* spp.), along the shoreline with their bases submerged. Always leave open passages that allow frogs to easily access and exit the water. To create even more biological complexity, you can grow aquatic plants in the water section. To do this, add a layer of substrate (e.g., gravel, sand, or clay) to the floor of the water area, and plant with short aquatic plants such as dwarf *Sagittaria (S. subulata* var. dwarf).

Aquaria

Hypothetically, aquaria for aquatic amphibians should be set up in the same manner as aquaria for fish. However, unless you want to keep very large species of fish or amphibians, there is only one way to design aquaria: create a natural-looking biological system using biological filtration and live plants to maintain water quality. Step-by-step details for this technique are provided here:

Step 1. Choose tank size and animal density

Because amphibians vary in proportion, it is difficult to provide specific guidelines based on size. A very general guideline is that the tank should have a length at least four times the length of the largest animal. For example, a 3-inch-long newt needs a tank at least 12 inches long. A general guideline for animal population is to provide a minimum of 1 gallon of tank space for every 2 inches of animal. Generally, a lower density of animals reduces biological waste, which makes water quality easier to maintain.

Step 2. Add substrate

Prior to introduction, thoroughly rinse the substrate to remove dirt and dust. At the bottom of the tank, place a 1.5- to 2-inch layer of coarse aquarium sand or fine aquarium gravel (up to a 0.5-inch diameter) or a fired clay substrate. Do not use fine silica sand, which is too dense for adequate root penetration, and do not use coarse gravel, which is too thick for good rooting.

Step 3. Furnish with rocks, wood, and cork bark

Next, add landscape structures, such as fresh water driftwood, rock, or cork bark. Aquarium stores usually carry a good selection of rock and wood suitable for use in tanks, while reptile supply stores usually carry cork bark.

To achieve aesthetic uniformity, select one kind of wood or rock that resembles what is found in nature. Use only wood and rock with smooth edges to reduce the risk of injury to the aquarium inhabitants. The rock and wood should cover less than a third of the surface area of the tank.

Usually just a few pieces are adequate as background or as a centerpiece around which plants can be arranged.

Much of the wood sold in aquarium stores leaches tannins when initially introduced into tanks. These tannins turn water the color of tea. It might be necessary to change the water many times over the first weeks or months to reduce the level of leached tannins to a point where the water is relatively clear. An alternative is to soak the wood in a large tub of water for several weeks prior to introduction.

Cork bark should be weighted down, glued to the tank sides with silicone, or wedged between the sides of an aquarium. It also leaches tannins, but only for a relatively short period of time.

Cork bark and drift wood should be soaked in tubs of water prior to use to clear them of dust and debris, and to allow tannins to leach out.

Step 4. Add plants

Plant heavily when you set up a tank rather than gradually adding plants over an extended period of time. This speeds up the time required for the tank to become balanced and biologically active. One advantage of a heavily planted tank is that the plants use excess nutrients in the water, leaving little available for algae growth.

Island Aquaria

Island aquaria consist of a tank that holds at least 10 gallons of water, preferably more, with the water level at least 3 inches below the top of the tank and one or two land areas emerging from the water. Because the structures used to construct islands take up space, larger aquaria are better suited for this type of design. You can use freshwater driftwood or rock to create the islands or attach panes of glass or acrylic (with silicone) to create underwater towers. As an alternative to islands, you can add a shelf by attaching a panel of glass or Plexiglas, to the back or sides of the tank using silicone. As with an aquarium, the water area needs to have good filtration and live plants. With island aquaria, large sponge filters or submersible filters are most effective because the low water level is unsuited for external, hanging-type power filters.

Island aquaria are half-filled tanks with islands made of stacked wood or rocks or wedged cork bark.

Plant Selection

Because most aquatic amphibians do not like bright lights, you will do best with aquatic plants that thrive in low to moderate light levels; many are listed on the next page.

Background Plants

These plants are likely to grow as tall as the height of your aquarium, creating a beautiful, naturalistic background. In some designs, you can place one or more tall plants in the

middle of the floor plan to add another visual dimension to the tank. Newts and frogs will use tall plants for climbing or resting near the water surface and also as egg-laying sites. Among the best choices tested and proven with the species in this book are: water wisteria *(Hygrophila difformis)*, elodea *(E. Densa)*, *Sagittaria* spp. (*S. subulata, S. graminea,* and others), *Vallisneria* spp. (the ribbon-leafed *V. spiralis* and the twisted-leafed *V. tortifolia*), large Amazon swords, and tall *Cryptocoryne* spp. *(C. balansae, C. ciliata, C. retrospiralis)*.

With bunch-type stem plants, such as water wisteria and elodea, regular pruning and pinching keeps plants controlled and bushy. Insert the cut sections in gravel to produce additional plants. Rosette- or ribbon-forming plants, such as *Sagittaria* spp., *Vallisneria* spp., and sword plants, will produce runners.

Midlevel Plants

These plants typically grow a quarter to half the height of the aquarium and are best planted in the middle areas of the floor substrate. Good species are medium *Cryptocoryne* (*C. affinis* and *C. blassii*), medium *Sagittaria* spp., smaller sword plants, and *Anubias* spp. (*A. afzelii, A. barteri* subspecies and varieties, and *A. gracilis*).

Foreground Plants

Plants for the tank foreground must be small so that they do not block the view. Most commonly used species spread by runners and form a short, green, growing carpet. The best is dwarf *Sagittaria* sp., which performs exceptionally well in my tanks. Dwarf sword plants (*E. tenellus* and *E. quadricostatus*) require more light but also thrive. The smallest of the genus *Cryptocoryne*, such as the dwarf forms of *C. nevillii* and *C. wendtii*, are good choices and eventually give the appearance of a tall grass field. Although there are many other good foreground plants sold in aquarium stores, most require bright lights and are unsuitable for a majority of the amphibians covered here.

More Underwater Plants

Two great low-light plants that thrive with aquatic amphibians under a variety of conditions are Java moss *(Vesicularia dubyana)* and Java fern. Both are varieties of epiphytes (plants that grow on other plants) and flourish if attached to wood or porous rock with fishing line or black thread. They make outstanding background or middle-ground plants. To remain looking its best, Java fern requires regular removal of old sections and replanting with new growth because the leaves have a limited lifespan.

The aquatic section of this floating frog setup shows various aquatic plants. This enclosure would also be ideal for various newts.

Because it is fast growing, Java moss needs to be harvested on a regular basis to prevent it from invading the entire habitat. The African water fern *(Bolbitis heudeloti)* is another underwater fern that is readily available and sports attractive cut leaves. It also grows best when attached to wood in the tank.

Filtration

To filter shallow water, use a sponge (foam) filter that is powered by an air pump, readily available in most specialized aquarium and reptile stores. Plastic foam filters perform consistently well in both small and large tanks. My personal favorites of the commercial products are the Tetra Billi sponge filters. These units are powered by air pumps, with the plastic sponge acting as a mechanical filter (trapping fine particulate matter in its cells) and as a biological filter (with the bacteria colonizing the cell spaces and breaking down ammonia and nitrites). Generally, you should provide filtration with at least an air-powered sponge filter whenever water is deep enough (3 inches minimum if you cut down the outlet tube).

Foam filters are my first choice for large tanks (I use large custom units equipped with power heads), but I also recommend an external power filter that combines mechanical (foam pad), chemical (activated carbon), and biological (e.g., biowheels) filtration. These filters prove particularly useful for tanks containing large amphibians that eat large amounts and quickly foul their water, such as axolotls and African clawed frogs. If using a sponge filter, cut back the outlet using a fine saw so it is just below the water surface.

Air pump-driven sponge filters are inexpensive and very effective filters for water sections of gravel bed vivaria. Remove the sponge filter every one to two weeks and squeeze the waste into a bucket of water. Do not try to thoroughly clean or rinse the sponge filter because its effectiveness comes from the bacteria colonizing the foam cells. In deeper shoreline tanks with at least 2.5 inches of water, you can use thin motor-driven submersible filters.

This sponge filter has an outlet stem cut to accommodate the shallow depth of a shoreline vivarium. Sponge filters are powered by aquarium air pumps and are ideal for shoreline vivaria and smaller aquaria.

In larger setups, use a miniature water pump with the outflow tube pouring over the gravel layer, which serves as a biological filter bed. Because water pumps generate heat, they are not recommended in small setups due to the risk of overheating the water.

Biological Filtration

Biological filtration is a process whereby biological organisms remove or neutralize waste matter, pollutants, or toxins

Miniature submersible power filters can be very effective in shoreline vivaria and smaller aquaria. This small unit has effectively filtered the water section in a 4- by 2-foot shoreline setup for three years.

A small water pump carries water from the water section over and through the gravel section of this shore-line vivarium. Sponge filters are powered by aquarium air pumps and are ideal for shoreline vivaria and smaller aquaria.

from a liquid, usually water. In closed systems, such as aquaria and vivariums, the process usually refers to filtration by nitrifying bacteria, which break down ammonia (NH_3) from animal waste into nitrite (NO_2) and then nitrite into nitrate (NO_3). Nitrate is less toxic to animals than ammonia or nitrite but can still accumulate to toxic levels unless water is changed on a regular basis. Most aquarium biological filters aim to provide high surface areas on which these nitrifying bacteria can attach and form biofilms. Plants can also play a role in biological filtration by providing surface areas and utilizing ammonia as a nutrient.

Lighting

For aquarium illumination and plant health, use two fluorescent bulbs running the length of the tank. For species that tolerate higher temperatures, such as floating frogs and clawed frogs, use incandescent lighting. I have had success growing certain aquatic plants (such as *Sagittaria* spp., *Cryptocoryne* spp., elodea, Java moss, Java fern, and hornwort) using a single 20-watt halogen bulb in small 2-gallon tanks housing dwarf underwater frogs and floating frogs.

Heating

Most of the species in this book do well at cool to moderate room temperatures, so additional heating is not required.

Some exceptions are floating frogs and clawed frogs, which prefer higher temperatures (in the upper 70s° F).

In setups using incandescent or halogen bulbs, the heat generated by these bulbs is usually enough to maintain desired temperatures. If not, try submersible aquarium heaters with built-in thermostatic controls, available in a range of wattage and sizes. Estimate approximately 5 watts per gallon.

Aging

Everyone working with planted aquaria finds that there is an aging cycle. Initially, problems are common because biological cycles have not yet been established. It takes three to six weeks for conditions to stabilize. This time frame allows nitrifying bacteria to build up to high enough levels that ammonia and nitrites are broken down. It also takes at least six weeks for plants to establish by anchoring into the substrate and increasing root mass and body mass. Once they spread their roots and achieve a certain density, aquatic plants effectively take nutrients from the water, limiting food available for algae.

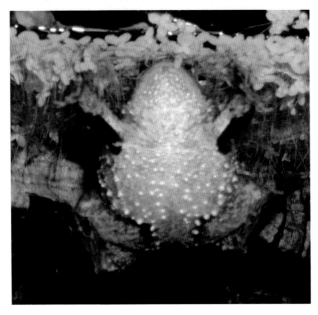

A ventral view of a floating frog shows the tubercled and intricately textured belly.

After this biological balance sets in, the tank takes a sudden turn. The water suddenly becomes clearer and the algae level starts to drop. A key to balancing a planted aquarium is the number of plants. As an example, I originally had two axolotls, a Hong Kong fire-bellied newt, and various fish in a 29-gallon, sparsely planted tank, and it worked well for two years. I added two axolotls, and in time, the plants, the inner surfaces of the tank, and the substrate became covered with algae. Determined to solve the problem biologically, I removed one axolotl, which led to a slight improvement—slowed growth of algae—but the problem persisted. I doubled the number of plants in the setup. Within a few weeks, the algae cleared and the tank was in equilibrium. The same pattern occurred with my tanks of paddle-tailed newts. I had a chronic problem with algae until I added plants and a couple of American flag fish, a species that is very effective at controlling hair algae.

Maintenance

The secret to a long-term successful aquarium is regular maintenance with a weekly to biweekly water change—probably the single most important procedure. Water changes stabilize the composition of the water, add minerals and trace elements, and remove fecal matter and plant debris from the aquarium floor.

As a general rule, every one to two weeks, siphon and replace 25 to 50 percent of the tank water. During siphoning, make sure to remove the biological waste that accumulates on the tank floor. The standard method for changing water is to remove it using an aquarium siphon and 5-gallon bucket.

Do not start a siphon using your mouth. There is a high risk of bacterial and parasitic infections because you can't avoid taking in the fouled water from the end of the siphon tube, and you may accidentally swallow it.

Siphons with hand pumps are sold at aquarium stores. Manual boat bilge pumps (which are very effective) and industrial wet-dry vacuum cleaners (being careful not to wet electrical parts or to accidentally suction frogs or newts) are also very effective.

Remember to dechlorinate the replacement water. This means buying a chlorine remover at a store that sells aquarium supplies or allowing water to sit in a container for at least twenty-four hours prior to use. In areas where chloramine (a compound of nitrogen and chlorine) is used to treat your water, a dechloraminator, also available from pet stores, should be added to the water. If you keep larval amphibians, leave replacement water in a bucket or tub for at least twenty-four hours before use to let dissolved gasses to dissipate.

Every one to two weeks, clean out filters and/or replace filter media and scrape algae off the sides using a single-edge razor or an algae-scraping tool. Also remove or prune overgrown or dead plants. Wipe dust off the tank cover and the unplugged fluorescent bulb, and clean stains and dirt off the outside of the tank. You can safely use window cleaner such as Windex on the *outside* glass.

If properly set up and maintained, planted tanks last for years, possibly more than a decade, without requiring a full disassembly, cleaning, and reassembly. I keep several 1.5-gallon setups, heavily planted and stocked with underwater frogs and floating frogs, that are three years old and look better than ever. My larger axolotl and newt setups are going into their fourth year and look the best they ever have.

CHAPTER 4
WATER

I f you plan to keep amphibians, water quality is one of the most important aspects of care. The ability to absorb water and a variety of water-soluble substances through their skin makes amphibians particularly sensitive to water quality and water-dissolved toxins. Larval forms, in particular, have especially fine epithelial (outer surface) skin, making them extremely sensitive to water chemistry and dissolved substances.

For example, water with high levels of chlorine destroys the fine gills of small amphibian larvae, damages their skin, and often kills them. Toxins such as ammonia, nitrites, cleaning compounds, and disinfectants pass through the skin and kill both adults and larval amphibians. High levels of dissolved gasses also penetrate the skin of tadpoles or larval salamanders and can lead to the formation of gas bubbles in their bodies that can kill them. Thousands of amphibians die annually because of improper or poor water conditions.

As you can see, the importance of water quality cannot be overemphasized. If you consistently have problems keeping amphibians alive, check the water quality first.

Aerosols and Pesticide Strips

Certain amphibians die when exposed to chemicals in aerosol forms, including cleaning compounds and hair sprays. Insecticidal pest strips (used by reptile keepers for treating mites) affect amphibians, and, when used in close quarters, might kill frogs and salamanders.

Detecting Water Problems

Amphibians in life-threatening water conditions show clear behaviors that things are not right. Life-threatening conditions include water that is too warm, too acidic, too hard, or too high in ammonia, nitrites, or toxins. The most obvious sign of distress is the animal's frantic struggle to escape the life-threatening environment. Many amphibians in life-threatening water swim at the surface of the aquarium and attempt to access a land area. You also might see spastic twitching, leg extensions, and panicked darting or swimming. If you see these signs, immediately remove your amphibians and replace the water (not from the same source).

Ideally, you should transfer animals behaving in this manner to a different tank with fresh, high-quality water. Then you should try to find out what is wrong with your setup. Start by testing the water for ammonia and nitrites (which are toxic at relatively low concentrations). You can test pH, but it seldom changes to a degree that is harmful to most amphibians. Regular water changes are a good way to avoid many of the problems associated with water quality.

Water Quality Guidelines

As a rule, adults of all species covered in this book are reasonably hardy and will tolerate a range of water conditions as long as the water is dechlorinated. If your tap water is considered of good drinking quality, an aquarium dechlorinator should be enough to make it suitable. If in doubt, request reports from your water treatment plant as to the chemistry of your tap water and its suitability as drinking water. If you have well or spring water and find that you have poor results with amphibians, have your water tested. One relatively inexpensive way to chemically filter your water is to run it through an activated carbon filter.

Water pH

Water pH is a measurement of the concentration of hydrogen ions in water. The pH scale ranges from 0 to 14 and is considered a reverse logarithmic scale. It is a reverse scale because the higher the pH number, the lower the hydrogen ion concentration. It is logarithmic because there is a tenfold difference between number units; water with a pH of 6 has ten times the concentration of hydrogen ions as water with a pH of 7.

From a practical point of view, all you need to know is that water with a pH of 7 is considered neutral, water with a pH less than 7 is considered acidic, and water with a pH of more than 7 is considered alkaline. Most natural fresh water has a pH range of 6 to 9. Slightly alkaline water, 7.2 to 7.4, is ideal for most of the species covered in this book. Most will do well and breed in water with a pH range of 6.8 to 7.6, with several tolerating an even greater range of 6.5 to 8. If you are serious about working with or breeding a particular species, you will find it worth your while to get more detailed information on the pH of the water in its natural habitat. Indeed, death of eggs or larvae of certain amphibian species often can be traced to water quality, including pH. Test kits are available through aquarium supply stores, allowing you to monitor the pH of your water. In naturalistic aquaria, regular testing is recommended because various biological processes tied to the release or absorption of carbon dioxide (such as bacterial decomposition and photosynthesis) can cause gradual pH shifts or cyclical pH fluctuations.

Dos and Don'ts of Purified and Distilled Water

Do not use reverse osmosis filtered water, purified water, or distilled water, which are all mineral-free, as a primary water source for the amphibians described in this book. You can, however, use these types of processed water for replacing evaporated water and for misting tanks, which prevents the accumulation of mineral stains on the sides of the tank and on plants.

Hardness

"Hardness" describes the level of dissolved mineral salts in water. Rainwater (condensed water vapor) is the original source of fresh water. Rainwater becomes slightly acidic on its way to earth because it reacts with carbon dioxide in the atmosphere to form carbonic acid. Once rainwater reaches land, it dissolves mineral salts as it flows through sedimentary rock and soils and, depending on the mineral makeup of the area, becomes gradually harder. Most water hardness forms when rainwater reacts with calcium carbonate (limestone) and magnesium carbonate to form bicarbonates; this is called carbonate hardness.

In general, amphibian keepers do not worry about hardness unless the water in their area has a reputation for leaving thick, visible mineral stains or for having high concentrations of certain minerals. Water with a high degree of hardness can affect the passage of materials through cell membranes, notably in fish and amphibian eggs. If you suspect that your problems are linked to water quality and hardness, purchase a water hardness test kit from an aquarium store or obtain a report on your water from your water treatment plant.

Also consider using bottled drinking water or mixing distilled or purified water with tap water to lower the mineral salt concentration. If a specific species of frog or salamander interests you, obtain information about the carbonate hardness and general hardness of their native waters.

Ammonia and Nitrites

In nature, fecal and excretory wastes in water undergo several stages of breakdown performed by various bacteria. Heterotrophic bacteria performs the first stage and yields ammonia, which is converted by nitrifying bacteria into nitrites and nitrates. Medium to high concentrations of ammonia and nitrites are very toxic to both fish and amphibians and should be carefully monitored. Nitrates, which plants use, are not as toxic but should be kept at low levels through regular water changes.

To prevent a buildup of these nitrogenous compounds, avoid overcrowding and overfeeding, provide biological filtration, and perform weekly water changes. The best way to monitor ammonia and nitrites in aquaria is to use test kits from tropical fish stores. The same guidelines used for fish will be applicable to aquatic amphibians.

Gas Bubble Disease

Sometimes tap water is supersaturated with gases, notably oxygen and nitrogen, which cause bubbles to form on the inside of a glass just filled with water. For amphibians, nitrogen is considered the more dangerous of the two because it causes gas bubble disease at lower concentrations. These supersaturated gases penetrate the amphibian's skin and form bubbles that can damage or kill tadpoles and salamander larvae, especially when the newly introduced water is warmer than the animal's body temperature. Gas bubble disease is a risk with all larval amphibians and with adults of some aquatic species. Keep an eye out for gas bubbles on the sides of an aquarium (or a glass of water), a good sign of unsafe levels, after water is introduced.

Signs of a stricken animal include floating at the top, visible bubbles beneath the skin, abnormal swimming patterns, and lesions under the skin. The damage caused by gases also exposes areas of the body to secondary infections. To prevent gas bubble disease, let water sit in an open container for at least a day.

CHAPTER 5

FEEDING

The information in this chapter provides general guidelines about feeding frogs and salamanders in captivity. The individual species accounts provide more specific details (see Chapters 6 & 7).

Land and Shoreline Amphibians

Land-dwelling frogs and salamanders in the wild primarily eat live prey—invertebrates, including numerous insects, pill bugs, and earthworms—which they identify as food by movement. These frogs and salamanders have earned a reputation for eating anything that moves and that fits in their mouths. Larger frogs, such as bullfrogs, also seize and eat small vertebrates such as fish, frogs, small reptiles, mammals, or birds. Unless you manage to train a frog or salamander to grab dead prey or meat strips from tweezers, you will need to find a source of live insects (specifically crickets) for land and shoreline species.

In captivity, commercially raised crickets provide the best basic diet for most amphibians and are available in several sizes through stores that sell reptiles. The length of the cricket should be from one-half to equal the width of the frog's or salamander's head.

Crickets purchased from a pet store might be under-fed and deficient in a number of vitamins and minerals required by amphibians. Before feeding them to pet amphibians, provide them with a nutritious diet. Most keepers house newly purchased crickets in one of the plastic terrariums sold through most pet stores and give them a commercial cricket-loading diet (many are available at your local reptile store) and freshly chopped greens and vegetables. An alternative diet consists of spirulina powder or flakes, tropical fish flakes, ground

These fire-bellied newts are feeding on frozen brine shrimp.

rodent chow, and pulverized cereals. Romaine lettuce, grated carrots, and orange slices provide both water and vitamins. After two or three days of this gourmet diet—when the crickets are nice and plump—feed them to your animals.

Supplementation

Even with this dietary boosting, crickets might be deficient in certain vitamins, minerals, and trace elements. To ensure nutritional value, lightly coat the crickets with a mix of powdered reptile vitamin/mineral supplement and calcium carbonate powder. Make the mix by combining one to two parts of powdered calcium carbonate with one part pow-

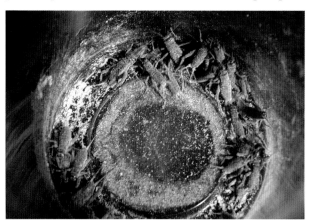

Prior to feeding them to your amphibians, place crickets in a jar with a small amount of a powdered vitamin/mineral powder. Perform this procedure twice a week.

dered reptile vitamin/mineral supplement. Both are available through reptile supply stores or through Internet suppliers.

Amphibian hobbyists lightly dust crickets before two to three feedings per week. To do this, place a small pinch of the mix in a jar, drop in the crickets, gently rotate the jar a few times until a fine dust covers the crickets, then drop them into the tank. If the crickets look like they have a thick powder coat, you added too much supplement and need to cut back to prevent risks of toxicity.

Other Foods

As part of a varied diet, offer other live prey to larger amphibians. Frogs and salamanders eat mealworms and waxworms but should receive them only in small amounts. Adult tiger salamanders and leopard frogs also eat larger king mealworms. These insects should be supplemented as indicated for crickets. Common garden worms, such as red wrigglers (not nightcrawlers), generally are relished, particularly by salamanders. You can collect them in gardens or buy

Superworms can be cut in half and used to feed large newts, axolotls, and common clawed frogs. Whole Superworms can be fed as part of varied diet to larger frogs and tiger salamanders.

them from fish bait stores. Several species of frogs, including fire-bellied toads and small leopard frogs, also eat pill bugs, which are high in calcium and found under rocks or wood. Large leopard frogs and tiger salamanders also take live pink (baby) mice. Tiger salamanders eventually learn to take food from tweezers, including pre-killed pink mice.

Aquatic Amphibians

A few frogs do not require live food, such as the common clawed frog and the dwarf clawed frog, making them ideal if you want to keep frogs without the hassle of live prey. Clawed frogs identify food by movement and scent, and eat both live and frozen foods as well as processed diets, such as trout chow, pelleted commercial foods, and shredded meat (lean beef or beef heart strips), or fish sections. The ability to keep clawed frogs without live foods makes them one of the most widely kept frogs in captivity.

Aquatic salamanders and salamander larvae, like clawed frogs, identify food by movement and scent. They feed on live prey as well as frozen and processed foods, such as bloodworms and slivers of lean meat or fish.

The length of a feeder cricket should be equal to the width of the head of the amphibian. Terrestrial amphibians tend to feed on live prey, while aquatic ones feed on both live and pre-killed crickets.

Pre-killed Insects

Aquatic amphibians quickly eat crickets and Superworms that have been killed by having their heads pinched. Smaller common clawed frogs and larger newts, such as Hong Kong fire-bellied newts and paddle-tailed newts, also take prekilled Superworms cut into sections. Some experts believe that Superworms cut into sections might be more digestible than whole Superworms.

CHAPTER 6

GUIDELINES FOR KEEPING POPULAR SPECIES OF TOADS AND FROGS

Oriental Fire-Bellied Toad *(Bombina orientalis)*

One of the most popular frogs in the world is the little gem known as the Oriental fire-bellied toad, a species now imported by the thousands from China and Korea. Its common name, fire-bellied toad, stems from its stout proportions, granular skin, and vivid red belly blotched in black. These attractive and hardy frogs are ideal for beginners, being tolerant of a range of conditions and thriving on live, commercially bred crickets.

Systematics: Fire-bellied toads are not true toads. These frogs were recently separated from the disc-tongue frogs

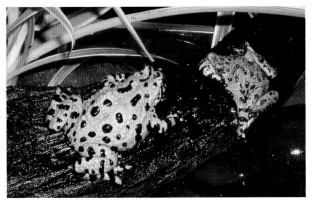

Korean specimens (left) of the Oriental fire-bellied toad *(Bom. orientalis)* tend to be larger than Chinese specimens, with crisp dark spots that contrast sharply with their bright green background color.

(Discoglossidae) and placed in their own family, Bombinatoridae, which includes six species of fire-bellied toads *(Bombina* spp.*)* and two species of water toads *(Barbourula* spp.*)*. Recent work showing a close affiliation of fire-bellied toads to painted frogs *(Discoglossus* spp.*)* suggests that inclusion in the family Discoglosside might be valid. In contrast to fire-bellied toads, which are semiterrestrial, water toads are relatively large, completely aquatic and lacking in bright ventral (belly) coloration.

Systematics

Systematics: the classification of organisms based on their characteristics, variation, relationships to other species, and evolutionary relationships.

Distribution and Origin of Imports: The Oriental fire-bellied toad occurs in the southern part of the Russian Far East, northeastern China, and Korea. Other species of fire-bellied toads are found in Europe, North Africa, Russia, China, and northern Vietnam.

Oriental fire-bellied toads sold in the pet trade primarily come from China and Korea. According to importers, the ones collected in northeast China are smaller and less brightly colored than those collected and exported from South Korea. Another fire-bellied toad imported from China and incorrectly sold as the "bronze morph" is actually a different species than *Bom. orientalis.*

This species is often sold as the bronze morph of the Oriental fire-bellied toad, but it is very likely one of the other Chinese species, possibly *Bom. fortinuptialis.*

Size: Oriental fire-bellied toads grow up to two inches long.

Longevity: Captive-bred and captive-raised Oriental fire-bellied toads can live up to sixteen years, and there are claims of individuals living more than twenty years.

Compared to imports (right), captive fire-bellied toads often become obese. In addition, their belly coloration tends to fade if their diet is not supplemented with a source of carotenes.

Sexing: You cannot determine the sex of a fire bellied-toad from its appearance outside of the breeding season. If you're lucky, you might witness a male call (a soft *oo, oo, oo* sound) or an attempt to grasp a female around the waist area (termed amplexus), two reliable indicators of gender. If a group of fire-bellied toads in a tank are in breeding condition, a close examination might help determine their sex. Breeding males develop black nuptial (mating) pads on the insides of the thumb, second finger, and forearms, as well as on the feet.

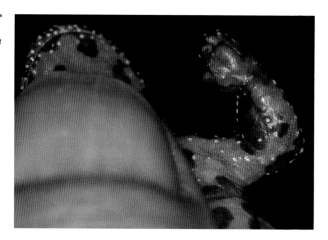

When in breeding, male Oriental fire-bellied toads develop dark nuptial pads on their forearms.

Selection: Oriental fire-bellied toads are a tough bunch; most imports arrive thin but in reasonably good shape. To pick out potentially healthy specimens, look for active individuals with rounded bodies and clear eyes. Avoid those with well-defined pelvic outlines or backbones and deeply hollow abdomens.

Because the sick toads are too weak to maintain a normal body posture (with the front part of their body raised), sick individuals often remain near horizontal when standing in shallow water. They hold their front and back at about the same level with the nostrils, which barely break the surface of the water. These listless, horizontal specimens typically die within a few days.

Purchasing several fire-bellied toads (at least half a dozen) results in a much more interesting vivarium than purchasing a single specimen. It greatly increases the likelihood of seeing at least one or two individuals at any given time.

Enclosures: The minimum enclosure size for up to four fire-bellied toads is a 10-gallon vivarium with a screen top. A 20-gallon tank or larger holds six or more animals and makes a more interesting display.

- *Shoreline vivaria*: These semiaquatic frogs are best kept in shoreline vivaria (see Housing). Make sure you have open areas of water/land interface for easy access to and from the water area.

- *Island vivaria*: Although it would not be my first choice as a system for keeping these frogs, small groups can fare well in aquaria with up to 6 inches of water and islands made of stacked rocks or large sections of driftwood. Fire-bellied toads will live happily enough on the emersed land areas (those that are above water). This system works best in relatively large tanks at least 24 inches long with one or more islands providing at least 6 by 4 inches of above-water surface and it allows you to combine the frogs with small fish species. The sizeable volume of water also helps maintain water quality.

- *Forest vivaria*: This kind of system allows you to include terrestrial or arboreal herps such as anoles, geckos, forest skinks, and treefrogs. For these setups, place a layer of drainage substrate such as pea gravel or, preferably, expanded clay pellets used in hydroponics on the bottom of the tank. Next, add a layer of peat-based potting soil with no perlite and no fertilizer or pesticide additives. Bury a shallow water container or plastic food storage container (at least 4 by 6 inches) into the substrate. Plant the land area with a variety of vivarium plants and landscape it with cork bark, wood, and rock. Use a sponge filter run by an air pump or a thin submersible power filter (such as a Duetto filter) to maintain water quality in the container. Enthusiasts who already have a tropical forest vivarium and wish to add frogs usually adopt this method. In this setup, keeping the small volume of water in the shallow container clean can be problematic; you must regularly remove the container to clean it and replace the water.

Feeding: Adult fire-bellied toads eat a diet of three- to four-week-old commercially raised crickets. To gauge the right size prey, make sure the length of each cricket is no greater than the width of the frog's head. Baby fire-bellied toads can be raised on fruit flies or pinhead to week-old crickets.

Adults accept a variety of other prey, including small waxworms and earthworms. They even learn to take nonliving food, such as strips of raw beef or fish, from tweezers. You need to supplement the diet twice a week by lightly dusting food with a reptile vitamin-mineral powder that contains calcium. Failure to supplement the diet—particularly with calcium—can result in metabolic bone disease (see Diseases and Disorders).

Behavior and Special Adaptations: Fire-bellied toads, like many frogs, should not be placed in or near your mouth or eaten. They produce skin toxins that taste foul and could be harmful. If you touch your eyes when handling these frogs, you will experience a strong burning sensation. If this should happen, be sure to rinse your eyes with water immediately. You will also experience a burning sensation in any cuts or bruises that come into contact with a frog. Always wash your hands after handling these frogs.

The vivid orange or red belly coloration of this species is considered aposematic, meaning it serves to warn birds and other potential predators of its foul taste and toxicity.

In fire-bellied toads bred, raised, or kept long-term in captivity, the belly coloration often fades to yellow-tan or yellow-orange instead of being bright red. The skin pigment cells responsible for the bright belly coloration have vesicles for storing carotenoids, plant-derived red and yellow pigments (including carotenes and xanthophylls). To develop the bright red belly coloration, feed your crickets grated carrots or color-enhancing fish flakes that contain canthaxanthin (a type of xanthophyll) several hours prior to feeding them to your frogs.

European fire-bellied toads *(Bom. bombina)* (left) are more patterned than yellow fire-bellied toads *(Bom. variegata).* Both species are sporadically available as imports.

The European fire-bellied toad *(Bom. bombina)* appears a dull-colored little creature until it exposes its vivid and intricately patterned belly.

The variation in the ventral color of fire-bellied toads collected in the wild can be, to a degree, attributed to the availability of xanthophylls in their habitat. This explains why some wild-caught fire-bellied toads have more orange bellies and others have red bellies. Manipulating xanthophyll pigments in the diet allows you to experiment with skin color in your fire-bellied toads.

When threatened, fire-bellied toads perform an unusual behavior that biologists describe as the Unken reflex. The toads arch their backs downward and raise the palms and soles of their feet to expose their brightly colored bellies. In some cases, the frogs go one step further and flip upside down to expose their colorful bellies. If turned right side up, the tendency to perform this behavior is sometimes so strong that they flip upside-down again. Amphibians performing the Unken reflex typically produce toxic skin secretions and have bright ventral warning colors.

Breeding: Under intensive rearing conditions, Oriental fire-bellied toads reach sexual maturity as early as nine months of age but usually do so after about twelve months. One of the easiest frogs to breed in captivity, the Oriental fire-bellied toad often breeds spontaneously in the spring and summer when kept indoors, even without special effort.

For more consistent breeding, the recommended pre-breeding conditioning is to cool the frogs to the 60s° F and reduce the photoperiod to only ten hours of light per day for at least two months. Generally, the cooling period follows the normal cooling trend of climate in a given area, which can be as early as October for northern temperate regions (many herpetoculturists cool down their animals from November 1 to March 1). After this period, return the frogs to normal temperatures and a longer photoperiod (fourteen hours of light a day).

Breeding begins when males emit a soft *oo oo oo* call. Receptive females move toward the calling males, who attempt amplexus. In these frogs, amplexus is performed around the pelvic (hip) region.

Females ready to breed remain in a normal posture with their hind legs withdrawn toward the body. Nonreceptive females grabbed by males extend their hind legs and perform silent release calls, felt as body vibrations, to indicate their unwillingness to breed. The extended hind legs of unreceptive females make it difficult for males to retain their grips, and the pairs eventually separate.

Breeding usually occurs in the evening, with females releasing eggs as males eject seminal fluid and sperm to fertilize them. This species might breed several times during the warm months of the year.

Young females (first-year breeders) produce small clutches of sixty to eighty eggs, but older females can produce up to two hundred eggs that adhere to plants and landscape structures. If you want to raise tadpoles, remove adults from the breeding tank. The tadpoles begin hatching by the third day. For two to three days, the tadpoles hang attached to the sides of the tank or vegetation, still using stored yolk. When they begin free-swimming and start feeding, powdered tropical fish flakes typically work well. After about a month, the tadpoles complete metamorphosis and climb onto immersed plants or the shore. Provide surface plants or ramps to give the emerging froglets access to land.

The yellow fire-bellied toad *(Bom. variegata)* displays an incredible pattern on its belly. Hardiness and ease of breeding make this species very appealing to hobbyists.

Initially dark gray with grayish white bellies, the froglets begin to feed on fruit flies and baby crickets a few days after metamorphosis is completed. Adult coloration appears in twelve to fourteen weeks.

Related Species: Yellow fire-bellied toads *(Bom. variegata)* are occasionally imported and sporadically available as captive-bred babies. They make attractive displays in shoreline or island aquaria with sizeable water sections and are often active during the day. It is quite a sight to see several of these frogs hanging suspended in the water and exposing their bright yellow and blue-black bellies. This species breeds easily if cooled into the 40s° F for two to three months during the winter.

Sometimes available as imports or captive-bred animals, the European fire-bellied toad *(Bom. bombina)* appears similar to the yellow fire-bellied toad, except that it has an orange or red belly. It is considered somewhat difficult to breed and requires a cooler hibernation period, as low as 38- 40° F.

The most bizarre and impressive of the fire-bellied toads is the textured, heavily warted giant fire-bellied toad *(Bom. maxima)* from southwestern China and northern Vietnam. With a dark gray green back and mostly solid red belly, it reaches a length up to 3.5 inches. The giant fire-bellied toad is rarely imported into the United States and even more rarely bred by hobbyists. It does best at comfortable room temperatures and has been bred following a period of cooling into the 50s° F.

Mixing Species: In larger tanks (standard 55-gallon or larger), you can include other species with fire-bellied toads, as long as at least half the surface area is dedicated to a land area and planted with a variety of plants rising near the top of the tank. Because these frogs can be secretive in planted vivaria, adding other species can make the habitat a more interesting display. Green anoles, small day geckos, and treefrogs can be kept with fire-bellied toads because they occupy a different ecological niche in the vivarium. Species active during the day, such as anoles and day geckos, are a good balance with these frogs. However, animal density should be small. Always quarantine new animals for thirty to sixty days before introducing them to the vivarium.

Water Toads (*Barbourula* spp.)

For reasons that are not clear, the common name "jungle toad" was chosen to describe the two species in the genus *Barbourula*. I prefer the name "water toad" because it is more descriptive.

Water toads deserve mention simply because they are rare and relatively unknown. The species *Bar. kalimantensis* appears in Borneo, and the species *Bar. busuangensis* lives in the Philippines. The Philippine water toad *(Bar. busuangensis)* grows to about 4 inches and is found in lowland rivers and streams that run through forests.

Like fire-bellied toads, water toads appear flattened, but they have many different attributes, including webbed hands, eyes that angle upwards, and a strictly aquatic life. Stomach analyses revealed that they feed primarily on aquatic organisms. They also lack the bright ventral coloration of fire-bellied toads—their bellies are described as a uniform dirty white. Nothing is known of the breeding habits of these rare frogs.

Floating frog *(Occidozyga lima)*

Take a bullfrog, put it in a turbo-powered shrinking chamber, and it would look just like a floating frog. The most charming feature of this species is its small size. Floating frogs make ideal pets for anyone who wants to

Because of their small size, hardiness, and tendency to remain in the open, floating frogs are ideal for small or large planted aquaria.

own a bullfrog but doesn't have much space. They offer the opportunity to design a miniature version of the vivarium theme of "frogs in a pond." I rank them among the best vivarium frogs because of what can be accomplished with their displays.

Systematics: Floating frogs, like bullfrogs and leopard frogs, are true frogs, placed in the subfamily Raninae of the family Ranidae. Their genus *Occidozyga* contains nine species.

Distribution and Origin of Imports: Frogs of the genus *Occidozyga* are found from southern China to India, the Philippines, and the Greater and Lesser Sunda Islands to as far as Flores. Floating frogs are found in a variety of water sources, including small streams, ponds, ditches, and rice paddies. Most of the floating frogs currently sold in the pet trade are *Occidozyga lima* imported from China.

Size: These tiny frogs only grow from 0.75 to 1 inch in length.

Longevity: They can live up to three years and possibly longer.

Sexing: Females are slightly larger and heavier bodied than males. By buying both smaller and larger frogs, you likely will end up with pairs. Close inspection of individuals may reveal the orange tan color of the males' throats. Females have white throats.

Selection: This species is commonly imported from China in fairly good condition. If you select active individuals with round bodies and clear eyes, most will establish well in captivity.

A ventral view of a floating frog shows the tubercled and intricately textured belly.

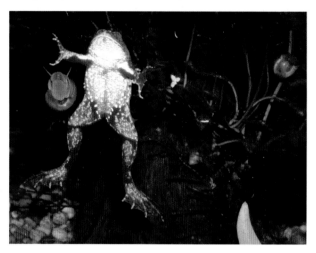

In general, purchase small groups of these tiny frogs—five or more rather than one or two. This creates a more interesting display and provides the opportunity to see breeding behaviors. Up to fifteen frogs can be kept in a 10-gallon aquarium.

Enclosures: These aquatic frogs fare well in enclosures as small as a 2-gallon aquarium or glass cookie jar. Up to five of these frogs can be kept in such small enclosures. A 10-gallon or larger aquarium allows you to create a fascinating and complex little ecosystem that incorporates these surface-dwellers. If you keep the water level at about half the tank height and if plants or wood sections emerge high above the water, you won't need a screen cover. Screen covers are, however, a good place to rest light fixtures and provide excellent protection from pets and children.

To give character to enclosures only half-filled with water, place a 1.5-inch layer of aquarium sand on the bottom. Add a small section of aquarium driftwood or rocks toward the back and sides with one or two landscape islands penetrating the front section.

Then place short plants at the base of the landscape structures. In the background, good choices for plants include elodea, water wisteria, and Java fern. Good choices for midlevel plants include smaller *Cryptocoryne* and *Anubias.* Attach small Java fern growths to wood, or insert them in natural cavities in the wood. You also can place some Java moss on wood. In the open areas in front of the tank, dwarf *Sagittaria* spp. or pygmy sword plants *(E. tenellus)* make a nice ground cover.

As an experiment, I planted a dwarf water lily in the sand substrate at the bottom of a floating frog setup lit by two fluorescent bulbs. Much to my pleasant surprise, the water lily thrived, and I was able to recreate a scene of frogs resting on lily pads. Unfortunately, the water lily did too well and produced so many pads that they risked covering the entire surface. I controlled the situation by using scissors to cut back the number of pads so that they covered no more than half the water surface. I also removed the offsets and planted them in other tanks. If you plan to try this, select the smallest tropical water lily you can find and plant it in a tank with at least 12 inches of water, preferably more. Water lilies typically die back in the winter, and the tubers (swollen underground stems) should be kept in moist moss in a cool area.

In ideal setups, floating frogs use plants reaching the water surface as resting areas. Floating frogs with no wood or plant resting areas spend excessive energy trying to remain on the water surface and eventually become stressed and more susceptible to disease.

Feeding: These frogs require small, live prey to thrive. Ideal foods include fruit flies and one- to two-week-old crickets, supplemented twice a week by dusting with a powdered reptile vitamin mineral supplement. They also feed on

small aquatic organisms that get close to the surface, including bloodworms (if placed at the water's edge) and small fish, such as young guppies or mosquito fish. Offer food three times a week to adults.

Behaviors: As befits their name, these frogs spend extend-ed periods of time at the surface of the water, floating or resting among plants or on the edges of land areas. They are generally cautious and, unless they become used to the captive environment, will readily perform their most com-mon defensive behavior: darting to the bottom of the tank.

Breeding: If cooled down into the 60s° F for two to three months, floating frogs breed in captivity. (Generally, the cool-ing period follows the normal cooling trend of climate in a given area, which can be as early as October for northern tem-perate regions.) They often breed even if their keepers do not manipulate temperature. They might breed at any time of the year, laying several hundred tiny eggs among vegetation.

Mixing Species: Floating frogs' small size makes them ideal for keeping with other small animals and for creating miniature ecosystems. However, if you intend to breed them, keep them by themselves so that fish and other potential predators do not eat their eggs before they can be collected and transferred to rearing containers.

For display purposes, several kinds of small fish can live well with floating frogs, including white clouds, guppies, white-cheeked gobies, and otocinclus algae eaters. You can even include dwarf underwater frogs, strictly aquatic species that spend extended periods of time on the tank bottom and thrive in setups for floating frogs.

Other species that can thrive with these tiny frogs include freshwater shrimp and ramshorn snails. In large shoreline vivaria, small treefrogs, anoles, and small geckos can coexist with floating frogs.

The Northern leopard frog (*R. pipiens*) spends extensive periods of time on land and does best in shoreline vivaria or island aquariums with a large land section. You must provide adequate levels of calcium in the diet as well as vitamin D_3.

Leopard Frogs (*Rana pipiens* and *R. sphenocephala*)

Leopard frogs, named for their high-contrast spotting, are some of the most frequently encountered frogs in the U. S. They are commonly found near bodies of water as well as in fields and meadows. "Leopard frog" is a common name for a complex of several species. In the pet trade, the most frequently offered species is the northern leopard frog *(R. pipiens)*. Occasionally, southern leopard frogs *(R. sphenocephala)* are also available.

Systematics: Leopard frogs are some of the better-known representatives of true frogs and are placed in the subfamily Raninae of the family Ranidae.

Distribution: Leopard frogs are found throughout most of the United States, except the West Coast. Having a wide distribution, populations show significant variations in pattern and color. Mutations, notably albinos, are of particular interest to hobbyists. Unfortunately, attempts to establish and commercially produce albino morphs have failed.

Size: Leopard frogs typically achieve lengths between 2 and 3.5 inches. Some individuals pass the 4-inch mark, with the record for the southern leopard frog being 5 inches.

Longevity: Leopard frogs seldom live long when kept indoors, in part because of the failure to provide a basking site and UV light source. They can live at least ten years when kept in outdoor vivaria or greenhouses.

Sexing: In *R. pipiens* and *R. sphenocephala*, males are difficult to distinguish from females except when calling, which exposes males' paired vocal sacs.

Selection: Both tadpoles and adult leopard frogs are commonly offered in the general pet trade.

Enclosures: Leopard frogs require relatively large enclosures to survive in captivity, at least a 20-gallon tank, preferably something larger. They can be kept either in shallow shoreline vivarium with a large land area or in a woodland vivarium with large open areas and a sizeable water container. Their setups can be landscaped with plants and driftwood, but it is critical to provide large open areas that include a basking site where temperatures reach into the low to mid 80s° F.

Leopard frogs are mostly active during the day, and they like to bask in sunlight. For this reason, provide them with an open area that includes a basking site and spotlight for heat.

Leopard frogs also benefit from some UV-B exposure, so, ideally, provide a full-spectrum or reptile UV-B fluorescent. When using a UV-B generating reptile bulb, always provide a shaded area to allow leopard frogs the opportunity to avoid exposure when they choose. Alternatively, place the frogs in screen cages or outdoor vivaria and allow them to bask in natural sunlight for a couple hours a week, making sure you provide shade, shelter, and a water container for them.

Leopard frog tadpoles are best raised in aquaria or plastic tubs filled with dechlorinated, aged water and fast growing plants, such as elodea. Because most tadpoles are at least partially vegetarian, avoid soft-leafed aquatic plants, which get damaged. Tough plants, such as *Anubias* spp. and Java fern, fare reasonably well in decorated tadpole setups. As food, tropical fish flakes, boiled romaine, and soaked alfalfa pellets are suitable for tadpoles. For good growth, feed no more than what can be eaten in about ten minutes, two to three times a day. You must perform partial water changes with aged dechlorinated water, one or more times a week, depending on the enclosure size.

Newly metamorphosed and adult leopard frogs are not considered the easiest frogs to maintain in captivity for long periods, although their needs are easily met with a little attention to vivarium design and diet.

Feeding: Unlike bullfrogs, which need to swallow food underwater, leopard frogs capture and eat live prey on land. Like most frogs, they attempt to eat any animal that moves and fits into their mouths. Leopard frogs can be fed crickets supplemented with a vitamin-mineral supplement that includes calcium. You can also offer supplemented mealworms in small amounts, earthworms, and the occasional pink mouse.

Behaviors: Leopard frogs are often active during the day, and they thermoregulate by basking. They are also wary and hide at the least sign of a potential threat. Your vivarium design should provide plant cover, and the enclosure should be in an area with regular activity if you want these frogs spending more time in the open.

Breeding: The indoor captive breeding and rearing of leopard frogs is not economically viable for hobbyists because of the space and labor required to rear the tadpoles. Techniques for artificial induction of ovulation and artificial insemination are detailed in laboratory reference books, such as *Amphibians: Guidelines for Breeding, Care and Management of Laboratory Animals.* If kept in an outdoor vivarium or greenhouse with a pool or pond, the leopard frogs will readily breed in the spring after a period of winter cooling. The frogs lay several thousand eggs and require a large water area for the tadpoles.

Mixing Species: Like most ranids, leopard frogs try to eat whatever moves and fits in their mouth. They are generally best kept by themselves.

Rice paddy frogs are hardy but secretive candidates for shoreline vivaria.

Rice Paddy Frog *(R. limnocharis)*

Rice paddy frogs are common inhabitants of rice fields, streamsides, and shallow ponds of parts of Asia and Indonesia. They have recently been imported in some numbers for the pet trade, probably to make up for the declining availability of leopard frogs.

Distribution and Origin of Imports: Imports hail primarily from China. This species also occurs in Pakistan,

India, Sri Lanka, southern Japan, the Philippines, and parts of Indonesia.

Size: Rice Paddy frogs reach up to 3 inches (7.6 cm).

Sexing: Males are smaller than females and have black throats.

The green-back frog, a ranid with small toe pads at its fingertips, readily climbs landscape structures, and, like certain treefrogs, tends to climb when the barometric pressure drops prior to rain.

Enclosures: This semiaquatic species is commonly found on the edge of ponds and streams. It fares well in heated shoreline vivaria kept in the mid to upper 70s° F during the day with a small temperature drop at night. Although hardy, this species tends to be wary and secretive and spends extended periods of time hidden during the day if provided with shelters.

Feeding: Rice paddy frogs fare well on supplemented crickets.

Green-Back Frog *(R. erythraea)*
This is a very pretty species with graceful lines and long hind limbs. It is mostly green with high contrast cream white dorso-lateral folds. Recently, it has been imported in increasing numbers for the pet trade.

Systematics: Green-back frogs are classified in the family Ranidae.

Distribution and Origin of Imports: Green-back frogs are found in Java, Borneo, parts of the Philippines, southern Vietnam, Thailand, Burma, and parts of India.

Size: Large females can grow up to 3 inches (7.6 cm).

Longevity: In the wild, this species is said to live about four years, but it can live longer in captivity.

Sexing: Males are only about half the size of females.

Enclosures: The green-back frog is a rather skittish species best kept in shoreline vivaria, but it can fare well in island aquaria with sizeable land areas. Provide a shelter or area of moist moss during the acclimation period. Because it is a lowland tropical species, maintain temperatures in the mid to high 70s° F. The green-back frog is active both day and night and once established more readily sits in the open. Some keepers keep them in shelterless shoreline vivaria with good success. Full-spectrum light with UV-B is recommended.

Feeding: The species feeds readily on supplemented crickets.

Breeding: This fast-growing, quick-to-mature species reaches sexual maturity by nine months of age. In many areas, the green-back frog has no specific breeding season and might breed year-round. Females lay eggs in water among aquatic plants. The tadpoles metamorphose after about three months. Short generation time and year-round breeding make this species a good candidate for aquaculture for the pet trade.

Mixing Species: These frogs seem to fare well in enclosures also housing large treefrogs.

Dwarf clawed frogs (*H. boettgeri*) are ideal pets for small aquariums with at least a gallon of water. This is an example of a 1.5-gallon dwarf clawed frog setup, planted with dwarf *sagittaria*, *cryptocrynes*, Java fern plantlets and Java moss.

Dwarf Clawed Frogs (*Hymenochirus boettgeri* and *H. curtipes*)

Some reptiles and amphibians are so easy and enjoyable to keep that they are suitable pets for virtually anyone. Dwarf underwater frogs are such pets. Their main advantage is that they can be maintained on frozen foods available from pet stores, saving owners the hassle of providing live food.

Currently both species of dwarf clawed frog, *H. boettgeri* and *H. curtipes*, are imported on a regular basis and available in the aquarium trade. Their ease of care makes them ideal small pets.

The species are difficult to tell apart, but this is of minor importance to most hobbyists, except for those few interested in breeding and raising these frogs, which is a challenging task. *Hymenochirus boettgeri* has a larger eye, a brighter iris, smoother skin, and smaller spots than *H. curtipes*.

Systematics: Dwarf clawed frogs belong to the family Pipidae (tongueless frogs), which includes five genera: *Hymenochirus, Pipa, Pseudohymenochirus, Silurana* (tropical clawed frogs), and *Xenopus* (clawed frogs)—for a total of twenty-six species. All of the species are flattened and strictly aquatic.

Distribution and Origin of Imports: Dwarf clawed frogs are found in tropical West Africa.

Size: This species grows up to 1.4 inches long.

Longevity: Dwarf clawed frogs can live at least five years under proper conditions.

Sexing: Because these frogs are tiny, determining the sex requires close observation. The most reliable way to determine sex is to look closely behind the area corresponding to the armpits. In males, light colored, swollen post-axillary glands are visible. Because close observation might not be possible in a pet store, it's best to purchase at least a half-dozen of these frogs, which gives you a good chance of having at least one pair.

Selection: Tens of thousands of dwarf clawed frogs are imported and sold in the United States annually, and they are among the most popular species in the aquarium trade. Unfortunately, dwarf clawed frogs are often kept unfed or overcrowded for extended periods of time, so many imports are thin and/or diseased. As a rule, avoid underwater frogs that swim or lie immobile at the surface of the water. Avoid exceedingly thin specimens with sunken abdomens and well-defined outlines of the hip bones. Look for plump animals that are active on the aquarium floor. Because a single specimen of this small species will be lost and seldom seen in an aquarium setup, consider buying several at a time. A small group proves much more entertaining and enjoyable.

Enclosures: There are two ways of keeping dwarf clawed frogs—the dull way or the exciting way. The dull way is the method in which these frogs are often presented in

This dwarf clawed frog rests among surface plants with its snout just out of the water. Plants serve as anchors for many kinds of aquatic and semiaquatic frogs.

stores: lying on the floor of a bare tank, blending with the aquarium gravel and hidden in the corners. Unfortunately, some stores display dwarf clawed frogs in bare plastic terrariums containing a low level of water, basically marketing them as disposable living toys for children. This is a version of a bird kept in a small cage, which appears to be just sitting there, doing nothing most of the time, when in fact, it is social, exploratory, and investigative animal. Dwarf underwater frogs are no different and, in the right setup, are a lot of fun, bringing an experience of the natural world inside a home or office. They are also very economical.

Exciting setups for these neat underwater dwellers can be relatively small enclosures. We keep small groups in 1.5-gallon tanks (9-inch cube custom) and 2-gallon cookie jars, as well as larger aquarium-type setups. Like common clawed frogs, dwarf clawed frogs are found in still waters, so they are best kept with either air pump-driven filters or small external power filters that generate little current. Experts recommend including water plants in any setup. They will help show off your frogs and provide climbing and rest areas in the aquarium.

Feeding: Dwarf clawed frogs recognize food by its movement and scent, so they feed on both live and frozen foods.

Their eyes are located at the sides of the head and the snout is short and pointed, which allows them some ability for three-dimensional vision. They investigate the aquarium floor by vision and scent, looking and smelling for small prey. They use a suction method to capture food, sucking in both food and water, then expelling the water with their mouths partially closed to keep the food from getting out. A favorite and staple component of their diet should be frozen bloodworms supplemented with other foods, such as frozen or live brine shrimp, and live foods that can be swallowed whole (daphnia, mosquito larvae, and small baby fish). Restrict the amount of food to no more than what these frogs ingest at one time, because uneaten bloodworms and brine shrimp foul the water. Dwarf underwater frogs also feed on fish flakes but usually in insufficient quantity to keep good weight. The flakes tend to break up as the frogs perform their suck-and-expel feeding behaviors, dispersing bits of flake throughout the aquarium and polluting the water unless small fish are present to feed on the scraps. The famous and talented Japanese aquarist Takashi Amano claims that these frogs feed on water snails; indeed larger frogs may feed on tiny newborn snails. I have noticed that populations of ramshorn snails appear to be controlled in tanks with large underwater frogs, but not in tanks with snails of 0.25 inches or larger.

Behavior: Dwarf clawed frogs spend extended periods of time inactive on the bottom of a tank or hiding in shelters. They are more enjoyable if kept in small groups whose interactions increase their activity level.

Breeding: Dwarf clawed frogs need to be at least a year old and of adult size to be considered for breeding. Although they are among the easiest to breed of all frogs, they are also some of the more difficult to rear from the tadpole stage, in part because the tiny tadpoles need tiny live prey. Keeping single pairs in a 5- to 10-gallon tank with no aeration or filtration to disturb the eggs yields the best chance for breeding success. The water must be heated to 78–82° F.

These dwarf clawed frogs are in amplexus. Notice the armpit swellings that characterize males.

Breeding occurs regularly under these conditions as long as the frogs are fed large amounts of food, such as frozen black worms and brine shrimp, daily.

The first sign of breeding usually observed is pelvic amplexus (gripping the hip area). In the course of spawning, which consists of underwater somersaults, females typically lay about 450 eggs. Large females might lay larger clutches, up to 1,000 eggs. The eggs are tiny and float on the surface of the water. For success at raising large numbers of froglets, remove the parents to prevent predation. The eggs hatch in two to four days. One of the problems with rearing this species is that tadpoles feed pretty much in the same way as adults, by sucking in water and individual prey units. For such tiny tadpoles, this means providing protozoa, rotifers, and other microscopic organisms. The tadpoles are also sensitive to changes in water conditions and, as with many tadpoles, are at risk for gas bubble disease; therefore, allow all water to sit for at least twenty-four hours before adding it to their tank. Once the tadpoles have gained a little size, they can be reared on baby brine shrimp (eggs can be bought in aquarium stores) or small daphnia. As a rule, hobbyists find that the captive-raising of these frogs is tedious, frustrating, labor intensive, and barely worth the space and effort. Typically, few tadpoles make it to metamorphosis.

The standard method for rearing this species during the warm months consists of raising tadpoles in an outdoor container or small, plastic pool with various water plants and an introduced culture of daphnia. Cover the pond with wire mesh (0.25 inch) to prevent dragonflies (but not mosquitoes) from laying their eggs in the system, and let nature takes its course. Some tadpoles will make it, and you should end up with a few of your own captive-bred underwater frogs. The tadpole stage lasts about six weeks and fully formed froglets appear within seven to eight weeks. Froglets eat daphnia, small mosquito larvae, chopped bloodworms, either live or frozen baby brine shrimp, and fish flakes.

Recently, a hobbyist had success at rearing underwater frog tadpoles in the parent tank. The tank was a planted and unfiltered 5.5-gallon aquarium that also contained snails. After egg-laying, the parents were given regular feedings of frozen black worms. Powdered tropical fish flakes were added to feed the tadpoles. Twenty-five out of several hundred tadpoles made it to metamorphosis. There are many reasons why this method might have been successful. The unfiltered, planted, and "well-fed" setup that also housed snails might have allowed for high levels of rotifers and other microscopic organisms to thrive. The tadpoles might have fed from worm scraps broken off by adults in the course of feeding. The plants might have provided refuge for the tadpoles, and the well-fed parents—although they ate some of the tadpoles—spared enough so that others survived and reached the frog stage.

Mixing Species: If you want to combine dwarf clawed frogs with fish, select smaller nonaggressive fish species or risk your frogs being injured or eaten. Fish species that work well include white clouds, guppies, otocinclus, white-cheeked gobies, zebra, and leopard danios. We've also successfully kept small freshwater shrimp (usually short-lived) and ramshorn snails with these frogs.

Common Clawed Frog (Xenopus laevis)
Clawed frogs are African members of the family Pipidae, characterized by black, clawlike keratinized tips on the inner three toes. Like other pipids, these frogs are flattened and strictly aquatic. The common clawed frog is one of the

most readily available and most studied frogs in the world, used extensively in biological and medical research. At one time, this species was exported in large numbers from South Africa and served as a tool for pregnancy tests. The frogs were injected with the urine of a possibly pregnant woman. If the woman was pregnant, the hormone levels in her urine would cause a female frog to ovulate and lay eggs within twenty-four hours.

With a charmingly goofy look—eyes on the top of its head, a pudgy body, and a big, smiling mouth—the clawed frog is among the more popular amphibian pets. Clawed frogs' aquatic habits and high levels of activity also make them consistently good, captivating displays.

In most states, clawed frogs are standard fare in the aquarium trade, but some states, such as California, where released animals have become established in some areas, have outlawed ownership.

Distribution and Origin of Imports: Clawed frogs are widely distributed in sub-Saharan Africa. The common clawed frog is found from South Africa north to Kenya, Uganda, and northeast Zaire, and west to Cameroon. They have been introduced into parts of southern California and Arizona.

Size: Clawed frogs grow almost large enough to be called big frogs (the general criterion for big frogs is a 6-inch snout-to-vent length), with large females reaching just more than 5 inches in total body length.

Longevity: The longevity record for a captive common clawed frog is fifteen years.

Sexing: Female clawed frogs grow larger than males and have a puckered vent, formed by tiny papillae (protrusions). Males in breeding condition have nuptial pads on the insides of their forearms.

Selection: Although the genus *Xenopus* contains fourteen species, only the common clawed frog is readily available through the pet trade. Recently, hybrids with *X. borealis* and the smaller tropical clawed frog, *X. tropicalis,* have also become available, at least through research animal outlets. The care of these species is similar except that both *X. borealis* and *X. tropicalis* are less cold tolerant than *X. laevis.*

Enclosures: In the wild, clawed frogs are found in bodies of still water, such as ponds or pools, and even in stagnant water. Their ability to gulp air at the surface allows them to survive in water with little dissolved oxygen. For this reason, laboratories keep these frogs in tubs of low water that is changed frequently or with a flow-through system where water drips at one end and flows out the other. Their hardiness allows you to keep them in tanks with unfiltered water as long as you perform regular water changes. Although this tough species adapts to a wide range of water temperatures and conditions, it is intolerant of fouled water with high levels of ammonia and nitrites.

A general rule for housing clawed frogs is to allow at least 5 gallons of water per adult specimen, but for display purposes I recommend only one adult frog per 10 gallons. Their setups can be designed as described in the chapter on housing with a few adjustments. First, these frogs, although tolerant of a wide range of temperatures, fare best if kept in the upper 70s° F, so use a heater if temperatures are too cool.

In still and stagnant waters, their sensitive lateral line organs (visible as a row of notches running along their sides) allow them to detect tiny currents and current shifts caused by potential prey or predators. Some experienced keepers feel that if kept in water with a strong current, these frogs will become stressed because they will be on constant alert for predators or prey. For this reason, do not use high current generating devices such as power-heads or strong external power filters. Most keepers recommend air powered sponge filters with a low air flow rate (use an air-line valve) and small external power filters, particularly if you intend to house them with fish. Many hobbyists who keep "frog only" tanks use no filtration but meticulously perform regular water changes.

When landscaping your vivarium, do not use anything with sharp edges, such as angular rock or wood pieces, and be sure to provide large open areas of ground. The choice of aquatic plants deserves special attention. These powerful swimmers investigate the tank bottom for food using powerful thrusts of their hind legs along with a scooping action of the forearms, displacing or damaging most smaller or fine-leafed aquarium plants. In general, foreground plants will not survive. Good vivarium choices include tough-leaved plants of the genus *Anubias* and Java ferns, which can be tied to wood with fishing line. Larger Amazon sword plants and elodea, once anchored in substrate, will also hold up reasonably well.

In tanks half-filled with water, choose plants that can be grown with their base in water, such as umbrella plants *(Cyperus alternifolium)*, philodendron Xanadu, sweet flag, and some irises.

Clawed frogs eat a lot and defecate accordingly, which makes keeping their tanks clean a challenge. Larger setups with low densities of frogs eventually harbor nitrifying bacterial loads that can perform a significant level of biological filtration. However, in most home setups, the only way to maintain water quality is weekly water changes, during which you should be sure to remove any fecal scum that accumulates on the substrate surface.

Feeding: African clawed frogs are opportunistic carnivores that eat a wide range of foods, including tropical fish and turtle pellets, live invertebrates (crickets, mealworms, and earthworms), lean beef, live and dead fish, and fish sections. You can buy specially formulated pellets specifically for clawed frogs from biological supply companies. These frogs feed primarily underwater but also catch invertebrates and small vertebrates at the water's edge. They will try to eat any animal that is small enough to fit into their mouths.

Behavior: Like most pipid frogs, *Xenopus* spp. alternate between extended periods of inactivity resting on the bottom and brief bursts of activity.

Breeding: African clawed frogs are bred in quantity for the aquarium trade and for medical research. The easiest way to breed them is to do what is done in biological laboratories: inject them with gonadotropic hormones available through biological supply companies. Instructions for hormone-induced breeding are also available from these biological supply companies and on the Internet.

To breed these frogs naturally, you need to simulate natural conditions. Basically, warm up the water to around 85° F and slowly decrease the water level to simulate a warm period of drought for several weeks. After this warm dry period, add cool water to simulate a cooler rainy season. As with other pipid frogs, amplexus is inguinal (around the hip region). Females lay and scatter several hundred eggs. The tadpoles are filter feeders and can be raised on powdered baby fish foods or special diets available through biological supply companies. Feed tadpoles sparsely to prevent the fouling of water often associated with raising filter-feeding tadpoles. Perform partial water changes with aged dechlorinated water every one to two days. Depending on temperature, the tadpole stage lasts two to three months. Considering the availability and low price of pond-raised common clawed frogs in the pet trade, it makes little economic sense for hobbyists to breed this species.

Mixing Species: A tank containing only clawed frogs can be a little dull, and hobbyists who keep them in large aquaria (at least 30 gallons, allowing at least 10 gallons per frog) usually like to add medium-sized fish with a body length equal to double that of the clawed frogs. Avoid predatory or aggressive/territorial fish, such as many of the cichlids. Larger cyprinodonts and small-mouthed catfish, such as larger syndodontis or medium plecostomus, are usually compatible with these frogs.

Remember that adding large fish to a tank increases the bioload and the chance that ammonia or nitrites will reach toxic levels. Provide low-flow filtration (use an external power filter intended for half the size of your tank) and perform regular water changes. As with axolotls, introducing valuable fish is not recommended.

CHAPTER 7

GUIDELINES FOR KEEPING POPULAR SPECIES OF NEWTS AND SALAMANDERS

Fire-Bellied Newt (*Cynops orientalis*, *Cyn. pyrrhogaster*, and *Cyn. ensaticauda*)

All tailed amphibians with legs belong to the order Caudata, a group popularly called salamanders. Caudata consists of nine families of salamanders, containing about 355 species. "Newt" is the common name given to certain genera in the family Salamandridae that spend extended periods of time in water. Many newts undergo significant physical changes in the structure of the tail, the dorsal crest, and body glands during their aquatic breeding stage. In classification terms, all newts are salamanders, but not all salamanders are newts.

The most commonly imported species of fire-bellied newt is the Chinese fire-bellied newt *(Cyn. orientalis)*. More rarely, the Japanese *(Cyn. pyrrhogaster)* and gold dust *(Cyn. ensaticauda)* fire-bellied newts have been available. Although some writers have claimed that the Chinese fire-bellied newt is hardier and more tolerant of warm water than the Japanese fire-bellied newt, this has not been my experience. If they are not thin, fire-bellied newts usually acclimate well to captivity.

The subtle differences between the Chinese and the Japanese fire-bellied newts are obvious if you pay a little attention. The Chinese fire-bellied newt is slightly smaller and has a more flattened body and smoother skin than the Japanese fire-bellied newt. If specimens are not available for comparison, skin texture is the best clue. The Japanese fire-bellied newt has obviously granular skin while the Chinese fire-bellied newt's skin appears smooth.

Systematics: All newts are members of the family Salamandridae.

Distribution and origin: Japanese fire-bellied newts are from Japan. Oriental fire-bellied newts originate from east-central China.

Size: Oriental fire-bellied newts are typically 3 to 3.3 inches long. Japanese fire-bellied newts are larger and range from 3.5 to 5 inches long.

Longevity: Kept properly, these pretty newts have lived up to twenty-five years.

Sexing: During breeding, males display a swollen cloacal region, and their tail broadens, developing a threadlike tip.

Selection: Most fire-bellied newts are imported in fairly good health. Avoid very thin specimens or those with skin sores and/or clouded eyes.

Enclosures: Once established, the two most common causes of death of fire-bellied newts in captivity are escape, leading to dessication (drying out and dying), and excessive heat. Many captives die every year during summer heat waves. Cool room temperatures in the upper 60s and low 70s° F are desirable for keeping this species. The upper limits of tolerance is around 78° F. To keep the water and newt cool during warm periods, place tanks in cooler areas of the house (e.g., at floor level rather than on a counter), and add ice or place cool packs in their setups on a daily basis.

These newts are best displayed in island type vivaria or shoreline vivaria with at least 3 inches of water. Live plants are a great advantage in these setups, improving water quality and providing areas for the newts to climb and anchor themselves, as well as lay their adhesive eggs. Live plants will show aquatic newts at their best. Elodea is generally a good choice as a background plant and often used during egg-laying.

In shoreline and island vivaria, these newts are best displayed in deeper water where they will be able to swim and

Dwarf sword plant *(E. tenellus)* covers the floor of this fire-bellied newt setup.

display their brightly colored bellies. Because they do not tolerate warm temperatures, they are not good pets to have in warm climates.

Feeding: Fire-bellied newts eat a variety of dead and living foods, including live or frozen bloodworms, tubifex worms, brine shrimp, mosquito larvae, and daphnia. They will also take newt pellets and two-week-old crickets.

Behaviors: Fire-bellied newts are a salamander version of fire-bellied toads, bearing bright orange blotches on their bellies. As with fire-bellied toads, the purpose of this bright coloration is to warn potential predators of their toxicity. Fire-bellied newts are toxic and should never be eaten, swallowed, or fed to other animals. There is at least one report of a student swallowing a newt as a variation of the old "swallow a goldfish" initiation rite. The student died.

Interestingly, these newts have their own version of the Unken reflex. If threatened when on land, they arch their head and tail toward the back to expose the bright ventral coloration.

Breeding: These newts require two to three months of cooling into the 50s° F, followed by an increase in temperature just above 68° F, to breed. Japanese fire-bellied newts have extended breeding periods, laying one to sixteen eggs daily, for up to fifty days, for a total of up to 320 eggs. Eggs are attached individually to vegetation. If you notice eggs on plants, transfer the plants (either whole or in sections) to a separate rearing container with high-quality, aged water. Use an air pump-powered sponge filter for filtration. The eggs will hatch in two to three weeks, depending on water temperature.

Mixing Species: Fire-bellied newts do not mix well with the other species mentioned in this book, which, by contrast, thrive in warm temperatures. For display purposes, fire-bellied newts can be combined with certain small fish, such as white clouds, which are small and tolerate cool water.

Raising Newts and Salamanders

Raising newts and salamanders from newborn larvae is a tedious process. After egg-laying, remove either the parents or the eggs. Transfer plants and other landscape structures with eggs attached to a separate planted tank with aged water. The most difficult time will be the first four to six weeks of rearing larvae, when most species require tiny live foods, such as rotifers, newly hatched brine shrimp (eggs available from aquarium stores), newly hatched mosquito larvae, and small aquatic crustaceans, such as newborn daphnia or cyclops. Regular partial water changes are recommended, along with filtration with an air-powered foam filter. With terrestrial species, as larvae near metamorphosis, provide access to a land area. Once they are on land, offer them live foods appropriate for their size.

Giant Fire-Bellied Newt (*Paramesotriton* spp.)

Also known as crocodile newts, these large newts are imported in some numbers for the pet trade. Some people think Hong Kong fire-bellied newts (*P. hongkongensis*) are the only ones imported, but this is not true. Chinese (*P. chinensis* and *P. caudopunctatus*) and Vietnamese (*P. deloustali*) are also imported at times. The large size and

Giant fire-bellied newts are the second largest newt after the ribbed newt (*Pleurodeles waltli*). Their rough skin, bright bellies, and contrasting gold irises make them outstanding display species.

heavy-bodied proportions of these species, as well as their granular skin, gold eyes, and bright orange and black bellies, make them some of the best display salamanders.

Systematics: All newts are members of the family Salamandridae.

Distribution and Origin of Imports: These newts are found in China, Hong Kong, and northern Vietnam.

Size: Large specimens can reach up to 6 inches long.

Longevity: Giant fire-bellied newts typically live up to ten years under proper captive conditions.

Sexing: Males have a more bulbous, swollen vent than females.

Note the swollen vent on this male giant fire-bellied newt.

The vent of this female giant fire-bellied newt is more flush with the body than on a male's.

Selection: Although some claim that these impressive newts are difficult to keep alive, the main reason they do poorly is because they often arrive thin and diseased. If healthy, the giant fire-bellied newt is hardy, long-lived, and one of the most impressive newts available. I have a huge adult that has lived with a group of large axolotls for several years. I also have other long-lived adults that are housed in their own island vivarium. The trick to success is the initial acclimation process, which involves initial feedings then treatment for parasites and infections. To avoid problems, buy only specimens that have adequate weight and appear healthy. Properly acclimating these newts means keeping them individually in small tanks in high-quality water in the low to mid 70s° F. Offer food, such as black worms, small earthworms or sections of earthworm, and prekilled crickets, every two to three days. It is important to monitor the newts for feeding, weight gain, and possible signs of deterioration. If the newts eat but remain thin, first treat them orally with metronidazole (Flagyl). Declining, sickly newts usually need oral or injected antibiotics. Frequently, these treated newts get healthy and gain weight.

Giant fire-bellied newts fare well in planted aquaria. Males will display intraspecies aggression during the breeding season, biting bodies and heads. Identifying imports can be difficult. Hong Kong fire-bellied newts *(Paramesotriton hongkongensis)* tend to be have smoother skin when compared to the two other species regularly imported from China. Chinese newts *(P. chinensis)* have very granular textured skin with no spots on the tail. *Paramesotriton caudipunctatus* has dark spotting on the lighter tail area.

Enclosures: The minimum habitat size for a pair of these giant newts is a 20-gallon tank setup as a planted aquarium or island aquarium. In the winter, keep temperatures in the 60s° F. These species will not tolerate drastic cooling. Although some books recommend a land area for these species, I have had good luck keeping Hong Kong newts in an aquarium with no land access but with plants that allowed them to rest near the water surface.

Feeding: General care is similar to that listed for fire-bellied newts except that giant fire-bellied newts eat larger prey, including prekilled, sectioned Superworms, earthworms, and prekilled crickets.

Behaviors: Giant fire-bellied newts turn onto their backs, exposing their brightly colored bellies, in order to feign death.

Breeding: A two-month cooling period can trigger breeding in this species. Females lay about one hundred eggs, sometimes more with large specimens, and individually wrap each one in plants with their hind feet. If the tank does not contain the right kind of vegetation, eggs will be found adhered to plants, wood, and other landscape structures. Apply the general rules for rearing other newts and salamanders. The larval stage lasts six months or more depending on rearing temperatures.

Paddle-Tailed Newt (*Pachytriton breviceps* and *Pac. labiatus*)

As display animals, these impressive newts rank among the very best aquatic amphibians. Not only are they beautiful and active, but also have intriguing social behaviors including tail waving. Although their natural habitat is in the cool, swift-moving waters of mountain areas, they have proven among the hardiest and most adaptable newts in the pet market and readily tolerate still water at room temperature.

Paddle-tailed newts *(Pac. labiatus)* are among the hardiest and best display newts, tolerating temperatures between 42° and 82° F. Ideally, temperatures should be kept in the 60s and low 70s° F.

Systematics: All newts are members of the family Salamandridae.

Distribution and Origin of Imports: Paddle-tailed newts are native to China.

Size: These rather large newts grow up to 6.6 inches long.

Longevity: Paddle-tailed newts obtained as adults have survived more than six years in captivity.

Sexing: Tails of males are broader.

Selection: Many paddle-tailed newts are imported in a healthy state. Just follow commonsense guidelines in selection. Avoid animals that are thin, have clouded eyes or skin sores, or are inactive when touched.

Enclosures: These aquatic newts can be kept in planted aquariums year-round, with or without an island area. They prefer large areas of water and fare well in aquariums and island aquariums. They are tolerant of temperatures, from the 40s° up to 80° F. Most captives appreciate areas of stacked rocks and will spend extended periods of time in the shelters and caves formed by these structures. Polyurethane foam backgrounds with hollow caves are an ideal alternative for display. Some hobbyists have noted that males of this species can be territorial and will fight with members of both sexes if too many newts are kept together. Paddle-tailed newts are also among the best escape artists of any amphibian. The importance of a secure top cannot be overly emphasized.

Paddle-tailed newts have distinguishing, complex facial structures and bright belly coloration.

Feeding: The paddle-tailed newt is one of the most predatory newts. It consumes various invertebrates, live or dead, and actively hunts small fish. Medium-sized fish (about half the length of the newt) and swift, wary smaller fish, can be successfully kept with these newts if one can accept the loss of the slow, the weak, and the unwary.

This paddle-tailed newt is performing a tail-wagging behavior that serves both as a territorial and courtship display.

Behaviors: As with other toxic newts, paddle-tailed newts display orange ventral warning coloration.

Breeding: Although I've noted courtship in my animals, I haven't seen them breed. A period of cooling and the provision of caves would probably be required for successful captive breeding.

Mixing Species: Paddle-tailed newts are best kept by themselves or with fish about half their length. I have successfully kept a group with Hong Kong fire-bellied newts in large tubs (150 gallons). In one experiment, I successfully kept these newts with gold barbs and a small musk turtle that avoided them.

Red-Spotted Newt *(Notophthalmus v. viridescens)*

These pretty North American newts are interesting little creatures, with most populations characterized (along with some European newts of the genus *Triturus*) by an additional life stage and an additional metamorphosis, compared to other salamanders (see below). The attractive adults, bright green and spotted with bright orange red, are collected in large numbers for the pet trade.

Systematics: All newts are members of the family Salamandridae.

Distribution and Origin: Red-spotted newts are native to southeastern Canada and the eastern United States.

Size: These newts grow up to 4.8 inches long.

Longevity: Red-spotted newts can live at least seven years in the adult stage.

Sexing: The vent of males is more bulbous than that of females and becomes swollen during the breeding season. When in breeding condition, males also develop yellow green dorsal crests as well as nuptial excrescences on their hind limbs.

Selection: They are available with regularity during spring and summer in the pet trade.

Enclosures: Being primarily aquatic with periods of time spent on land, either island aquariums or shoreline vivaria are suitable for housing this species. As a display, island vivaria will generally allow for better observation and greater enjoyment. Depending on where they were collected, red-spotted newts are generally more tolerant of warm temperatures than are other species. They enjoy comfortable room temperatures in the 70s° F and tolerate winter temperature drops into the 40s° F.

Feeding: Efts (immature juvenile red-spotted newts), being terrestrial, require small live prey including fruit flies, springtails, white worms, bloodworms, and one- to two-week-old crickets. Aquatic adults will feed on live foods, including crustaceans (brine shrimp, daphnia), mosquito larvae, and bloodworms, as well as frozen foods, pelleted commercial newt diets, and low-fat canned dog food.

Behaviors: As seen in most salamanders, the embryonic stage is spent within an egg and is followed by a gilled larval stage spent in water. However, the larvae metamorphose into an intermediate yellow brown to bright orange red, immature land stage. The juveniles in this stage are called efts. After two to four years, the terrestrial efts, which have rounded tails, finally metamorphose into mature aquatic adult newts with laterally flattened tails.

Red-spotted newts wear their bright red warning spots on their backs. These newts are so toxic that few fish will eat them, making the survival rate of their offspring higher than most other amphibians. The major toxin produced by red-spotted newts is tetrodotoxin, the same deadly poison found in the infamous Japanese fugu puffer fish, relished as sushi and the cause of many deaths when not prepared in the right manner.

Breeding: If cooled drastically during the winter (for example, in an unheated garage) into the low to mid 40s° F for two to three months, this species can be bred in captivity. Females lay up to three hundred eggs individually or in clumps, either attached to vegetation or adhering to landscape structures. The tiny larvae require rotifers, tiny crustaceans, and other small invertebrates for successful rearing. Under ideal conditions, they metamorphose after three months into 1.25- to 1.5-inch terrestrial efts, which can be raised in shoreline vivaria on tiny crickets, springtails, large flightless fruit flies, white worms, and tubifex. The immature eft stage, during which these newts are colored yellow brown to pale orange, can last two to four years. In most populations, growth of this species occurs mostly during the eft stage, when the animal more than doubles in length. In some areas, where habitat is unsuitable for the eft stage, populations of this species follow the typical salamander pattern, with an extended gilled larval stage lasting up to two years before metamorphosing into an adult.

Mixing Species: Red-spotted newts are generally best kept by themselves.

FAQ: How can I obtain salamanders that are not standard pet trade fare?

If you are seriously interested in exotic salamanders, contact specialist dealers through the Internet or through ads in magazines, such as *Reptiles* or *Reptiles USA.* You'll find some of the more unusual species not typically available in the pet trade, including ribbed newts *(Pleurodeles waltli)*, the beautiful black and yellow European fire salamanders *(Salamandra salamandra)*, and tree salamanders (genus *Bolitoglossa*). Make sure you research their care requirements before purchasing them.

Three-Lined Salamander *(Eurycea longicauda guttolineata)*

This pretty, long-tailed brook salamander is one of the few members of the family Plethodontidae (lungless salamanders)

collected in substantial numbers and available (seasonally) in pet stores. It is semiaquatic and often found near the banks of ponds and streams, making it ideal in a shoreline vivarium.

Systematics: The three-lined salamander is the only commonly sold Plethodontid salamander in the pet trade. Members of this family of salamanders are commonly known as lungless salamanders because they lack lungs. Most of their breathing occurs through the skin and the lining of the mouth.

Distribution: These U.S. natives are found from Virginia to the Florida panhandle, and west to the Mississippi River.

Size: Three-lined salamanders grow up to 7.75 inches, two-thirds of which is tail.

Enclosures: Keep these salamanders in shoreline vivaria with a secure screen top. They are notorious escape artists, able to climb through even the tiniest cracks. Like many salamanders, they require cool, high-quality water in the 60s° F, although they will tolerate warmer temperatures (up to the low 70s° F). Provide cork bark shelters. Regrettably, most three-lined salamanders die prematurely in captivity because they are kept too warm and are not supplied with small live food.

Feeding: Three-lined salamanders feed on small moving invertebrates, which they capture by projecting their tongues. Offer them small crickets (one to two weeks old), larger fruit flies, live black worms, and white worms.

Breeding: Three-lined salamanders are not usually bred in captivity, but winter cooling is recommended if you plan to breed them. This species lays eggs in crevices formed by landscape structures in shallow water. In several *Eurycea* salamanders, parental care of eggs has been reported. The eggs hatch after six to eight weeks. After four to seven months, the tiny larvae metamorphose into tiny salamanders.

The thick head and stout proportions of normal-colored axolotls clearly distinguishes them from larval tiger salamanders.

Axolotl *(Ambystoma mexicanum)*

The axolotl is one of the best and most enjoyable aquatic amphibians for display. Its eye-catching appearance, hardiness, and entertaining activities makes it one of the most incredible vivarium animals available. Probably no other salamander can equal its droll facial expression. With its bizarre, almost embryonic appearance, the white axolotl is the most stunning of the bunch.

Systematics: Axolotls are strictly aquatic members of the family Ambystomidae and are closely related to tiger salamanders.

Distribution and Origin of Imports: These intriguing amphibians are found in Lake Xochimilco, Mexico where they are now considered threatened. Most captive specimens are descendants of wild stock imported decades ago into Europe.

Size: Axolotls grow to a length of 8 to 12 inches long.

Longevity: Axolotls maintained under proper conditions typically live for ten to fifteen years. However, the oldest axolotl on record lived twenty-five years.

Sexing: Males are less heavily bodied and less rounded than are females. Males also have a more bulbous vent, formed by caudal glands.

Selection: Although they are bred in large numbers for research, they are only sporadically available in the fish and pet trade.

Axolotls come in a range of colors and patterns. The wild form is black with green or yellow mottling. The most visually striking and readily available axolotls are leucistic specimens, which are pure white with black eyes and bright red gills. Also commonly available are the yellow albino axolotls, which have a bright, golden yellow background and red orange eyes. Other forms include white albinos, which resemble leucistics but have orange eyes instead of black, and the rare piebald black and white axolotls. You can find information on the genetics of the many mutants of axolotls in scientific literature and on the Internet.

Enclosures: Because axolotls are aquatic, they must be kept in aquaria of at least 20 gallons and preferably larger. My experiments indicate that about 7 gallons per adult is suitable for most systems. Although the bare tank laboratory method is often advocated for keeping this species, it is best displayed in planted aquaria with coarse aquarium sand on the bottom. In my setup, I use a base of cat litter (100-percent kiln fired clay) with a layer of decomposed granite

Few aquarium displays can beat a planted tank with a group of adult axolotls, especially any as incredible looking as this leucistic specimen.

sand on top. Good plant species include sword plants, *Vallisneria* spp., *Sagittaria* spp., *Cryptocoryne* spp., and elodea. A little more difficult to keep but feasible in larger axolotl setups are Java fern and Java moss attached to smooth driftwood. Under most household conditions, this species does not require additional heat, as it does best at cool room temperatures in the low 70s° F and enjoys drops in the 50s° and 60s° F during winter. Good water quality is critical, as axolotls are particularly sensitive to ammonia and nitrite concentrations. To maintain good water quality, add an external power filter that also provides a high level of biological filtration (such as biowheels or porous ceramic/glass filtration media). Another filtration alternative is a jumbo foam filter powered by a small power head. With filtered tanks, a partial water change every one to two weeks will usually keep high water quality and healthy inhabitants.

Feeding: Axolotls are gluttons. Good foods include prekilled, supplemented crickets and mealworms, floating trout chow or fish pellets, earthworms, and even occasional prekilled pink mice. A varied diet of these foods will keep axolotls healthy. They also may eat strips of fish, lean beef, and beef heart, but these foods are nutritionally deficient unless supplemented. Feed your axolotls every one to two days when young and two to three times a week as adults.

Behaviors: Closely related to tiger salamanders, axolotls are large neotenic salamanders. This means they can reproduce when still in a larval state. In fact, they never leave the larval state. Axolotls are among fourteen species of salamanders considered to be "obligate neotenes," meaning that they only exist as juveniles.

Breeding: Although their babies are a lot of work to raise, axolotls are probably the easiest salamanders to breed in captivity. The trick to successful breeding is to keep them cool (around 65° F), well-fed, and at a high photoperiod (fourteen hours of light per day). Breeding success is also increased by keeping individuals separated except at breeding time. Under these conditions, it is possible to have four to six breedings a year by pairing individuals every couple of months. I keep three pairs of axolotls together in a large tank setup in my garage that cools into the low 60s° F for two to three months in the winter. They usually breed twice a year, in early and late spring. In my setups, they lay eggs on plants and landscape structures. After eggs are deposited, I transfer plants and rock or wood with eggs attached to them to another established tank or to large tubs for hatching and rearing of the larvae. The eggs hatch in about two weeks.

Baby axolotls are initially small (about ⅜ of an inch) and limbless, feeding only on tiny live moving food, which makes them a chore to raise. Good foods for initiating feeding are live baby brine shrimp, which are easy to hatch from eggs available at aquarium stores. Simply follow the instructions provided with the eggs. Small mosquito larvae, cyclops, or daphnia also work. Baby axolotls should be offered as much food as they can eat once or twice a day for the first couple of months. By the time they are 1.5 inches long (about five weeks), baby axolotls will begin to more readily feed on nonliving foods such as chopped black worms (use a single-edge razor for chopping), frozen baby brine shrimp, and sinking baby fish pellets.

One of the problems with raising groups of baby axolotls is water quality. They are messy feeders, eating a lot and defecating accordingly. Under laboratory conditions and in small containers, axolotls need partial water changes. The water should be dechlorinated and aged at least 24 hours to allow gases to dissipate. I now raise babies in 150-gallon plastic tubs with elodea, siphoning wastes from the bottom and making a partial water change twice a week. When raised in groups and if not provided with enough food, all sizes of axolotls eat limbs and tails or cannibalize their smaller brothers and sisters. It is this trait that has made them undesirable to many stores that, when keeping a number of axolotls together, end up dealing with a large percentage of mutilated specimens. On the bright side, axolotls regenerate lost limbs and tail sections in just a few weeks once separated from the cannibalistic axolotls. They reach sexual maturity in just over a year.

Mixing Species: The general rule is that if it moves and looks bite-sized, or if it smells right and can be grabbed, an axolotl will try to eat it. On the other hand, larger fish will consider axolotls as potential food. Remember that the larvae of their close relatives, tiger salamanders, are commonly sold as bait. This imposes limitations on keeping axolotls with other species. If the recommended density of axolotls is reduced by a third (one adult axolotl per 10 gallons), axolotls can be combined successfully with small to medium sized fish (up to half an axolotl's length). In my 29-gallon setup, I have three axolotls, a group of cherry barbs, and a white-cheeked goby that have lived together for more than two years. In another

Axolotls can be kept with nonaggressive, medium-sized cool water fish, such as the Chinese sucker fish.

tank, I successfully combined white cloud minnows, gold barbs, and American flag fish with newts and axolotls. The typical scenario is a selective one. Some fish are smart enough to remain uneaten and others are not. As a rule, I wouldn't recommend mixing expensive fish with axolotls.

Waterdog (*Ambystoma tigrinum*, larval form)

Larval tiger salamanders are sold in large numbers through bait stores and the aquarium trade, being offered under the name "waterdogs." They resemble axolotls in general

Waterdogs are the larval form of the tiger salamander. They resemble axolotls and can be kept in the same manner.

appearance except for slightly wider and flatter heads, and a gray green sheen to their bodies.

Enclosure: They can be kept like axolotls up to the time of metamorphosis.

Behaviors: Several factors affect when these larvae will transform into adult tiger salamanders, including size, age, temperature, iodine content of their water, and diet. As the larva nears metamorphosis, its gills recede, the head narrows, becoming rounder, and the uniform skin color is replaced with the blotched adult pattern and color. Larvae ready to leave the water will frantically swim at the surface and should be transferred to a shoreline vivarium.

Tiger Salamander *(Ambystoma tigrinum)*
Ask salamander keepers what is the king of land-dwelling salamanders and most will say the tiger salamander, a large, beautiful and impressive beast that, unlike most salamanders, also displays a degree of responsiveness.

Systematics: There are six subspecies of this wide ranging U.S. species. The most attractive by far is the barred tiger salamander *(Ambystoma t. mavortium)* black with a crisp-edged, high-contrast cream to yellow barred pattern. Also

The barred tiger salamander is the prettiest of the tiger salamanders and well worth making a special effort to obtain. If you want a pet salamander, none is more responsive and outgoing than this species.

popular are eastern tiger salamanders *(A. t. tigrinum)*, which have black to chocolate brown backgrounds and olive green to yellow brown spots. Different populations vary in their color and pattern and serious hobbyists will make efforts to track down individuals with bright, crisp-edged spotting.

Distribution and Origin of Imports: Tiger salamanders are found throughout the U.S.

Size: At a potential total length of just over 13 inches, and growing large enough to consume pink mice, the tiger salamander is the largest land-dwelling salamander.

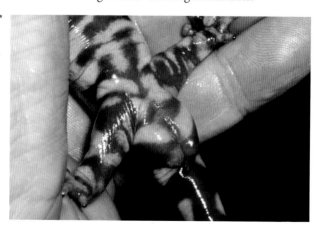

Like many other salamanders, male tiger salamanders have a swollen cloacal region that becomes more pronounced during the breeding season.

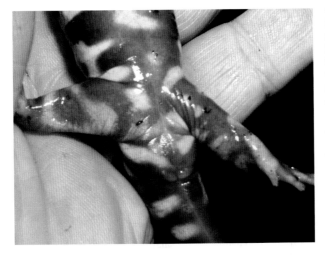

Female tiger salamanders have a vent that is more flush with the body than that of males.

Longevity: Under ideal conditions, tiger salamanders raised from larvae can live up to twenty years, possibly longer.

Sexing: Males have a bulbous, swollen vent, compared to females.

Selection: Most of the tiger salamanders offered for sale are healthy, although they often appear thin from being underfed. Avoid limp animals or those with clouded eyes.

Enclosures: Tiger salamanders are primarily available through bait stores and the aquarium trade in their larval forms called waterdogs, when they can be kept like axolotls.

As adults, tiger salamanders are land-dwellers except for their brief breeding season. Metamorphosed tiger salamanders fare well in shoreline vivaria at least 30 inches long, or in large woodland vivaria at least 24 inches long with a large water container. Make sure to provide them with a shelter. Because this species grows large, eats large amounts of food and defecates accordingly, pay special attention to keeping their water and substrate clean. Like most salamanders, tiger salamanders do best at cooler room temperatures. Although not required, winter cooling in the 50s° F combined with a fasting period can extend the life of captive tiger salamanders.

Feeding: Tiger salamanders try to eat anything that moves and can fit into their mouth. In captivity, foods include crickets, mealworms, earthworms, and pink mice. They should be fed two to three times a week. Insects should be lightly coated with a vitamin-mineral supplement prior to feeding. Because tiger salamanders are gluttonous creatures that tend to become obese in captivity, take care not to overfeed them.

Behaviors: Except for the breeding season, tiger salamanders are primarily terrestrial and nocturnal. In captivity, they quickly learn to associate the presence of an owner with food and will come out even during the day to feed.

Breeding: Considering the current value of these salamanders, it is not worthwhile to attempt indoor breeding of most forms of this species. Management of wild populations and creating ponds for aquaculture is a more viable and economically sound course than small-scale hobbyist breeding. Female tiger salamanders lay large numbers of eggs (totaling up to five thousand) and the task of raising any number of larvae to a sellable size is physically and economically unrealistic except under outdoor pond conditions.

CHAPTER 8

DISEASES AND DISORDERS

T he frogs and salamanders discussed in this book, if initially healthy, tend to be hardy and relatively long-lived. If your animals have fared well for many months and suddenly look sick, first evaluate their living conditions. Often enough, wrong temperatures, high levels of ammonia or nitrites in water, fouled soil, and stress factors, such as excessive light or overcrowding, contribute to illness and a depressed immune system. Correcting these factors often causes frogs or salamanders showing signs of illness to become healthy again.

If your animals continue to look or behave sick, consider veterinary care. Unfortunately, veterinary treatment can be very expensive. A basic exam costs many times the cost of a single frog or newt. Add the costs of cultures and medications combined with the real possibility that sick frogs or salamanders might die despite medical attention, and you might decide veterinary care is not a viable option. In any case, the animals in your care deserve humane treatment and should not be left to suffer without intervention nor should they be killed by inhumane methods such as freezing.

Disease Prevention

To ensure the good health and long life of your animals, you must carefully design and maintain a vivarium so that the temperature, light, water quality, topography, furnishing, and diet meet the needs of its inhabitants. Checking these conditions regularly will play a critical role in preventing the onset of disease in your animals. In addition, new animals must be quarantined prior to introducing them to a tank with established pets. Besides flaws in husbandry, the introduction of sick animals is probably the most significant cause of disease in established collections.

How to Recognize a Sick Amphibian

To recognize illness in the species covered in this book, look for the following signs:

1. *Inactivity or unusual behaviors.* The first thing you might notice is abnormal behavior or appearance. In fire-bellied toads, for example, inactivity and a horizontal posture (rather than the normal front-raised posture) are clear signs of illness. In salamanders, listlessness or struggling at the water surface indicate illness. With terrestrial amphibians, spending an inordinate amount of time in water is another sign of sickness.

2. *Gradual or sudden weight loss.* Signs of weight loss in frogs and salamanders appear in the abdominal area, which begins to look hollow, and eventually the outlines of the hip bones and backbones become apparent.

3. *Body/abdominal bloat.* This can be caused by excessive digestive gases associated with poor digestion caused by overeating, oversized prey, intestinal parasites, intestinal infection, respiratory infection, or gas bubble disease.

4. *Skin blotches.* The frog or salamander might display red blotches, caused by hemorrhaging, or white fuzzy blotches, caused by fungi.

5. *Eye cloudiness.* When a frog's or salamander's immune system is depressed, the integrity of the lens is often one of the first things affected by pathogens. Inappropriate water quality (such as too acidic or too hard) and high

The cloudy eyes of this recently imported fire-bellied toad indicate infection. Providing high-quality husbandry conditions, including a basking site, and treatment with antibiotics are necessary to cure this problem. If left untreated, specimens may end up blind even if they survive.

A well formed fecal sample of a fire-bellied toad. Undigested cricket parts also visible in the water are common in the feces of many amphibians. Specimens that do not produce formed feces may be parasitized.

levels of toxins in the water will also affect the lens. Cloudy eyes are usually secondary to other problems. In rare cases, trauma to the head and orbit can lead directly to an infection in the eye.

6. *Edema.* This is a general swelling of the body, head, or limbs. Various factors, from poor water quality to bacterial infections and kidney disease, can cause edema.

Crash Syndrome

A common problem in newly imported animals is a sudden decline soon after purchase, which is popularly known as crash syndrome. Some newly imported animals initially appear healthy and might remain that way for the first week or two weeks, but then crash, or become sick and die. Hobbyists experienced with this syndrome implement protocols that include quarantine of new animals and preventative treatment with parasiticides and antibiotics. One interpretation of the cause of this crash syndrome is that stress, overcrowding, and exposure to pathogens between capture and importation eventually taxes the animal's immune system until it finally starts to fail. As a result, varying percentages of animals become sick and die during their first weeks in captivity. This initial "die-off" occurs with many imported animals. The number of animals that die varies greatly and depends on the species and the conditions it faced between collection and its final home.

Isolate sick frogs and salamanders in simple, easy-to-maintain setups.

To help prevent crashes, the first step is to quarantine new purchases and to optimize environmental conditions, providing appropriate ranges of temperature and humidity, shelters, and regular feeding. The experienced hobbyist chooses two courses in dealing with potential crash syndrome. One is to wait and see what problems arise, addressing each problem as it appears. The other is a preventative approach, providing prophylactic treatment to newly acquired specimens with parasiticides and/or antibiotics. Because most of the species covered here tend to adjust well to captivity, the wait-and-see approach is recommended unless the animals already appear weakened and compromised.

Toxing Out

Frogs and salamanders absorb water through their skin and urinary bladders. If the water contains high concentrations of ammonia or other toxins, frogs and salamanders will display signs of poisoning from toxins, or "toxing out." The signs begin with hyperactivity, followed by lethargy in frogs, spastic extensions of the hind legs, and sometimes cloudy eyes. These frogs and salamanders eventually become listless and die, usually in a matter of a few days. As soon as these signs are noted, replace the water. With semiterrestrial amphibians, such as floating frogs, fire-bellied toads or newts, place the affected animals in shallow water (half the body height when at rest) in a separate container (a plastic storage box). This practice is important because toxed-out frogs and salamanders might be too weakened to move and may drown. Replace the water twice daily until improvement is noted, then return the animals to a setup with proper conditions. Toxing out can also occur if terrestrial frogs or salamanders absorb toxins from moist soil. Treatment is the same, except that the substrate in the vivarium will have to be replaced during treatment. A sign of fouled substrate is a bad smell, either a strong ammonia smell or simply a foul odor from decomposition or a buildup of fecal waste.

Parasites

It doesn't make economical sense to pay for veterinary checkups for parasites in an amphibian that you paid less than ten dollars for, so many hobbyists adopt a wait-and-see attitude. If a frog or salamander eats but loses weight, has watery feces, or is active but eats poorly, parasites are a

possible cause of disease. Obviously, the most effective way to address a potential parasite problem is to consult a qualified veterinarian and have a fecal exam performed. Another option is to buy a microscope along with books or manuals that give instructions for performing simple fecal exams.

Two groups of parasites are routinely treated by amphibian hobbyists. Nematode worms are easily treated with orally-administered fenbendazole (Panacur) at 100 milligrams (mg) per kilogram (kg), repeated in two weeks. Various flagellate protozoans and amoeba are treated with metronidazole at 100 mg per kg, repeated in two weeks. It is also effective against anaerobic bacteria. However, it should be noted that many amphibians normally harbor some flagellates as part of their typical intestinal flora, so treatment for these parasites is recommended only when a frog or salamander is showing signs of illness and flagellate numbers are unusually high. Because fenbendazole is also effective against certain flagellate protozoans (if administered daily for several days at half the recommended dosage), it is frequently used as a first course of parasite treatment. Often enough, home treatment for these parasites causes an improvement in frogs that fail to maintain weight and are just slightly ill. Ivermectin (Ivomec injected once subcutaneously at 0.2 mg per kg), another powerful parasiticide for treating nematodes, has also been used successfully orally, subcutaneously, and topically. However this potent drug must be dosed carefully because it has a narrow margin of safety.

Amphibians might also harbor tapeworms and flukes, but there is relatively little information available on effective treatment. Praziquantel (Droncit) has been used with some success to treat tapeworms in various amphibians and can be administered both orally and topically. Consult other hobbyists or a qualified veterinarian (very few are experienced with amphibians) before attempting home treatment with any parasiticide.

Velvet Disease

Velvet disease, a type of skin infection better known in fish, also infects aquatic amphibians. The gray, slightly fuzzy, discolored skin and gill patches associated with velvet disease can mislead you into believing the lesions are caused by a fungus. In fact, they are caused by the dinoflagellate protozoan parasite, *Oodinium pillularis*. Treatment consists of changing water, keeping temperatures toward the warm end of the ideal range, and bathing affected animals in salt baths (50 to 100 grams of sea salt per gallon for fifteen to thirty minutes daily). If the infection is extensive, administer an antibiotic to prevent secondary infections.

Bacterial Infections

Identifying bacteria as a cause of disease in amphibians is difficult without the help of a qualified veterinarian. Because of the costs involved, most hobbyists keeping just a few specimens treat sick animals with a broad-spectrum antibiotic and hope it works. Generally, bacteria is the cause of illness if the signs of decline are sudden, rather than gradual. These signs include inactivity, failure to feed, weight loss, cloudy eyes (if one has eliminated toxing-out syndrome), edema, and skin hemorrhaging. If these signs are noted, a first step is to reduce the risk of spreading an infection by transferring sick animals to a separate treatment container, such as a plastic terrarium.

Over-the-counter fish antibiotics, though readily available, are not always effective at treating amphibians when administered in water. With aquatic amphibians, sulfa-based fish medications have been used with varying degrees of success because they are readily absorbed through the skin. Other over-the-counter fish antibiotics used in baths are not very effective or have to be dosed at such a high level that they can cause other problems. For example, the proper concentration of tetracycline in a bath solution will damage the skin of amphibians. The route of administration also affects the speed of action. Many antibiotics act quickly if injected, while others are nearly as effective if administered orally.

One of the better-known bacterial diseases of frogs is called red-leg disease because of the subcutaneous hemorrhaging associated with the later stages of the disease. Red-leg disease is caused by bacteria of the genus *Aeromonas*. It can be treated with tetracycline at 50 mg per kg administered orally twice a day. Factors contributing to the onset of this disease, such as environmental stress from poor-quality water or exceedingly low temperatures, must be rectified. A general antibiotic that has proven effective for treating a variety of bacterial infections in amphibians is trimethoprim-sulfa, a prescription drug that is obtainable through your veterinarian. It is most effective if administered orally, but it can also be absorbed through the skin—either applied with a cotton swab or dissolved in a shallow level of water, such as a bath. Enrofloxacin (Baytril), an injectable and oral antibiotic that has proven effective against a range of bacterial infections, works at 5 mg per kg daily for seven days. Certain drug combinations that target both aerobic and anaerobic bacteria can also be very effective, such as metronidazole.

From a practical standpoint, communication with experienced amphibian keepers will often be the most effective method for deciding on treatment. When seeking treatment, veterinarians specialized in treating reptiles have the general background to effectively treat amphibians if they have the relevant references handy.

Viral Infections

The diagnosis and treatment of viral infections in amphibians is outside of the scope of the hobbyist. Nonetheless, hobbyists should be aware of the risks of transmitting viral disease and the importance of quarantine to help prevent the spread of such diseases.

Fungal Infections

If your amphibian has white, fuzzy patches on its skin, it probably has a fungal infection. Fungi are an important and ubiquitous component of nature. When healthy and kept in the proper environmental conditions, most amphibians at all life stages (egg, larva, adult) effectively fight off fungal infections. However, amphibians can fall victim to pathogenic fungi if stressed, kept at the wrong temperatures, kept in filthy or poor-quality water, subjected to skin abrasion or trauma, or weakened by disease. The most frequently encountered fungal disease in aquatic amphibians is saprolegniasis, an infection of the skin caused by fungi of the genus *Saprolegnia* and characterized by white, fuzzy skin patches. Treatment consists of rectifying stressful conditions and placing the infected animals in a salt bath (50 to 100 grams of sea salt per gallon) for fifteen to thirty minutes daily until the infection clears. Other fungal infections can be difficult to diagnose and even more difficult to treat. The key to preventing fungal infections is prevention by providing the proper living conditions.

Drug Dosage

There are currently few guidelines available for drug dosage in the veterinary treatment of amphibians. The two most practical references are a chapter by Kevin Wright, D.V.M., in *Reptile Medicine and Surgery*, edited by Douglas Mader, D.V.M., and *Amphibian Medicine and Husbandry*, the first practical reference on the veterinary treatment of amphibians, edited by Kevin Wright, D.V.M, and Brent Whitaker, D.V.M. Even with the latest references at hand, drug dosage and administration requires some competence, skills, and equipment. Many of the amphibians in this book weigh only a few grams, so you will need a gram scale to determine how much of a drug should be administered. You must also develop proficiency at metric conversions and dosage calculations. If you have several animals in the same size range, you can determine a more accurate per animal weight by weighing five or more animals together, then dividing by the number of animals.

The greatest difficulty in treating small amphibians comes from properly determining and administering the amount of drug required for treating a single animal. This is particularly true with drugs that have a narrow margin of safety. Drug dosage, which is typically in mg of drug per kg of body weight, needs to be calculated from the drug concentration of the product. For example, liquid Fenbendazole is typically sold at a concentration of 100 mg per ml (per cc). At a dosage of 100 mg per kg, treating a 2-gram newt or floating frog means effectively extracting $\frac{1}{500}$ of a cc, something not feasible with most dosing syringes. The only way to easily do this is to dilute drug products to lower concentrations when treating small amphibians. Liquids for dilution must be sterile if the drug is to be injected, and they must be compatible chemically with the particular drug. Besides the problems of proper drug dosage, another difficulty in treating small amphibians is drug administration. Injectable drugs are generally easily administered with tuberculin syringes, but oral drugs require careful opening of a tiny mouth—not always the easiest task. In general, small wedges with rounded tips cut from plastic deli container lids are the tool of choice for opening the mouths of small frogs and newts. These thin wedges can be easily inserted between the edges of a mouth to permit opening, allowing medication to be administered with a small syringe.

CHAPTER 9

MIXING SPECIES

To mix or not to mix species, the question divides hobbyists into two camps: the conservative purists who oppose the practice and the vivarists who find it a challenging area of experimentation. The correct answer for you depends on your goals. If your primary goal is to breed certain species of amphibians, there is no doubt that the single species approach is the most effective way to obtain consistently good results. Although it is possible to keep different amphibian species in greenhouse situations and have them reproduce successfully, this will usually not be the case when they are kept in smaller home vivaria. The presence of other species can increase your animals stress, interfere with reproduction behaviors, and put eggs or larvae at risk of being eaten or damaged. If your goal is not captive breeding but instead to create a complex and stimulating display, experimenting to increase species diversity in a vivarium will be a challenge and a source of great enjoyment.

Guidelines for Mixing Species

Quarantine: Different species harbor different parasites and bacterial flora. For this reason quarantining individual animals and treating parasites is generally recommended prior to combining them in the same enclosure. Although some experts warn about the dangers of cross infections when species are exposed to foreign pathogens, it appears that many species, even from different areas of the world, can cohabit for long periods within a vivarium. I have successfully kept frogs from Asia with frogs from Africa or the U. S., and lizards from the Americas with African and Asian species of amphibians and reptiles. If there are problems, they usually appear during the quarantine period.

Sick animals, no matter what the species, risk infecting healthy ones. So the first rule about mixing species is to quarantine all animals prior to introduction.

Similar Broad Environmental Requirements: When mixing ectotherms (cold-blooded animals), the second rule is that the species you intend to combine should have the same general environmental requirements, including habitat type, temperature range, and relative humidity. For example, mixing tropical frogs that prefer warm temperatures with temperate newts or salamanders that prefer cool temperatures does not usually work. You also cannot mix a land-dwelling species with a strictly aquatic one unless a vivarium is large enough to provide both environments. For obvious reasons, mixing species from arid areas with species from moist tropical forests is not wise.

Same General Head Width: With one or two exceptions, all adult amphibians are strict carnivores, and most prefer to feed on live prey. With many species of frogs and salamanders, if another animal smells right and moves, the larger animal will attempt to eat it—even if it's a member of the same species. As many studies have shown, mutilation and cannibalism are not uncommon in amphibians. In vivaria, a general rule that works reasonably well is that animals with a head width more or less equal (a difference of no more than 25 percent) can be safely mixed together. This is not true with all species of amphibians (e.g., juvenile horned frogs) but this guideline can be applied to most mentioned in this book.

Niche: In ecology, an important concept is *that of a species' niche*, which simply means its position in an ecological system. For a simplified example, dyeing poison frogs *(Dendrobates tinctorius)* are diurnal (active during the day), moist, tropical forest litter dwellers. They feed primarily on ants and other small arthropods, use skin toxins as a defense, and depend on bromeliads with water-holding centers for breeding. Their habits put them in minimal competition with species that are found in the same habitat but have different habits and requirements, such as nocturnal tree-dwelling treefrogs that feed on larger insects. As a general rule, two species cannot occupy the same niche in an ecosystem, although some niche factors can be shared and allow for what is called sympatry (occupying the same geographic areas without interbreeding). The concept of niche can be applied when combining animals in a vivarium. Species with different habits but the same general habitat requirements can be mixed. However, if species have the same habits, they will compete for space and resources.

In a vivarium, space can be landscaped and stratified to create various niches and allow mixing of different species. For example, cork bark slabs or hollow rocks at ground level will serve as shelters for species that like to hide during the day and come out in the evening. Introducing branches or foliage can provide rest and activity areas for nocturnal arboreal species such as treefrogs and diurnal *Anolis* spp. lizards. Climbing geckos, species that often prefer to cling to broad solid vertical surfaces, usually remain on the glass sides of a tank or on vertical bark slabs and, except for food, do not compete with most amphibians.

Vivarium Size and Low Densities: As mentioned in the previous section, limitations of space and resources restricts the number of animals that can be kept in a vivarium. Obviously, a large vivarium allows you to create a greater number of niches and thus makes it possible to mix several reptile and amphibian species. Alternatively, keeping a low density of animals relative to vivarium size and niche availability also allows you to successfully mix species.

Interestingly enough, for some territorial species, overcrowding to prevent individuals from establishing territories can sometimes allow mixing of species that would not be possible under other conditions. This practice is commonly performed by aquarium hobbyists who want to display a large number of territorial species, such as African cichlids. There is little information on this subject with aquatic amphibians, although it has been suggested that aggression between paddle-tailed newts is reduced under crowded conditions, which prevent individuals from establishing territories linked to breeding sites.

Some Tested Combinations: There are many combinations of reptiles and amphibians that can live together. The following are some combinations that have worked for me, with the length of time I have successfully kept them together noted in parentheses:

- *Floating frogs and dwarf clawed frogs with fish* (more than three years): Several kinds of small fish have survived about two years in my setups, including white clouds, otocinclus catfish, and guppies. Ghost shrimp, a short-lived species, have lasted several months and even successfully bred.

- *Fire-bellied toads, green anoles, Jamaican anoles, spiny reed frogs, gold dust day geckos* (five years with all species, two years with day gecko and still going)

- *Fire-bellied toads and green treefrogs* (more than two years): Provide a basking light to ensure health and proper conditions.

- *Paddle-tailed newts and Hong Kong fire-bellied newts* (more than two years): I tried this in 80-gallon tanks at low densities. It worked with regular feeding. I noticed newts with missing front feet from mutilation a few times, but they eventually grew back. Various fish have survived for varying periods of time. A white cloud lived for two years. A few gold barbs and American flagfish are still alive.

- *Axolotls and Hong Kong fire-bellied newts* (more than three years): I didn't think it would work, but for some reason this setup has been very successful. Low population densities and dense planting are recommended.

I've also had a mostly bottom-dwelling white-cheeked goby in the setup, which has surprisingly survived while dozens of other active free-swimming fish have been eaten. A cherry barb is still living after more than two years. In general, cool water fish fare well with these newts and salamanders. The Chinese sucker (*Myxocyprinus asiaticus*), which has high fins and an attractive pattern, is one of the more desirable species now available in the aquarium trade that survive with larger newts and axolotls. Plecostomus catfish have also subsisted with this species. Goldfish are said to pick at the gills and are not recommended.

CHAPTER 10

AMPHIBIAN VIVARIA IN THE WORK PLACE

B esides the obvious aesthetic appeal and stimulation provided by aquatic and semiaquatic vivaria, research shows that people who view aquaria can have health benefits, including production of a general state of relaxation and reduction of blood pressure. Desktop vivaria can offer a way to rest the eyes from long periods of staring at a computer monitor, as well as serve as a backdrop for creative thought and handling stressful work. Some claim to find inspiration in the dynamics of animals and plants in a vivarium. Others feel that their lives are enriched by caring for other lives, and that the setup of their tanks in some way keeps them connected to the more stable, slower-changing aspects of the natural world. Whatever arguments are presented, there is

This desktop display consists of an inverted floating candle bowl planted with cryptocorynes, dwarf sagittaria, and Java moss. It is illuminated by a desktop halogen and contains a pair of floating frogs and small guppies.

Floating frogs inhabit this floating candle bowl.

Glass globes 8 inches in diameter or larger are suitable for displaying underwater frogs, a pair of Oriental fire-bellied newts, or baby axolotls (until they grow too large).

An axolotl globe setup

strong anecdotal evidence that aquaria and vivaria can enrich the work place and provide uplifting decorative and psychological benefits.

Desktop Vivaria

Because of their limited size, small setups of 6 gallons or fewer are generally ideal for the desktop. Suitable enclosures include small tank systems, such as the innovative Eclipse line by Marineland, custom-made cube tanks, glass bowls, large cookie jars, and clear glass vases. Suitable species for these setups are correspondingly small ones, notably dwarf clawed frogs, floating frogs, Oriental fire-bellied newts, and various species of small fish. For maintenance, a bucket, aquarium siphon, and water bottle are essential. Also make sure that the desk area is clear of anything that can be damaged when changing water.

Larger Tanks

If asked what my favorite large tank display is, I'd have to say a planted axolotl setup with half a dozen specimens, including one or more morphs, along with various fish. I can't imagine anyone not being captivated by this kind of setup, and it would be ideal in an office setting. As a second choice, I'd recommend newt and fish combinations in island vivaria. In terms of maintenance, after the original setup, you can hire an aquarium maintenance service to come weekly or biweekly to perform the necessary water change and cleanup, including removal of algae from glass and replacement of filter media. These services are a tax-deductible expense when performed in the workplace.

If the aquarium lights are on timers, they can safely be left unattended over weekends, without any need for feeding the inhabitants. Just make sure you bring food on Monday.

CHAPTER 11

AMPHIBIAN VIVARIA AS EDUCATIONAL TOOLS

Vivaria often prove to be invaluable teaching tools. In the course of its ten years of existence, the now-defunct visionary organization American Federation of Herpetoculturists (AFH) was instrumental in the growth of the hobby, sponsoring and organizing a graduate course for teachers called "Herpetoculture in the Classroom." The mastermind behind the project was the AFH educational coordinator, Dan McCarron, a biology teacher in Rock Springs, Wyoming. For three summers, teachers gathered in Rock Springs and were instructed about keeping amphibians and reptiles in classrooms, and how to apply herpetoculture as a tool for teaching biology and addressing conservation issues. The course was taught by McCarron, Sean McKeown (author and former curator of reptiles at the Fresno Zoo), David Perlowin (author of popular books on kingsnakes and garter snakes), and myself. It provided the opportunity for a unique collaboration and exchange of ideas among peers. An emphasis was placed on vivarium design and the great potential this offered teachers for addressing important concepts of ecology and for leading to presentations related to physics and biology. The following are brief sources of ideas, inspired by "Herpetoculture in the Classroom," that will hopefully prove useful to both teachers and students:

- *Lighting:* The lighting used in vivaria offers teachers the opportunity to teach students about topics involving sunlight and the light spectrum, such as photons, light frequencies and the effects of different light frequencies (e.g., infrared and heat; ultraviolet radiation and UV-B range that allows humans and other animals to synthesize vitamin D_3; and the long-term effects of exposure to UV). Related topics include the role of the ozone layer in filtering ultraviolet radiation, and amphibian declines linked to increased UV exposure as a result of the deterioration of the ozone layer.

Well-designed vivaria are educational wonders that can include numerous species of plants, fish, amphibians, reptiles, and various invertebrates. They are ideal for teaching students about ecology, systems theory, and many other areas of biology.

- *Heat sources:* Classes could explore why the earth is warm; the critical role of the sun as a heat source and the origin of solar heat and radiation; the role of CO_2 and the greenhouse effect; and how heat is absorbed, stored, and reflected in nature.

- *Aquatic substrates:* Lessons could focus on the role of bacteria in the breakdown of biological wastes, the biology of bacteria, and the role of biofilms in aquatic environments. Students might study nitrifying bacteria, anaerobic bacteria, and the breakdown of nitrates, and they could examine conditions that can overload a biological system and lead to a breakdown of the aerobic bacterial layer. Substrates can also help explain the role of CO_2 released by bacteria and its effect in the ecosystem and use by plants.

- *Plants:* An entire course on botany can be based on plants in vivaria. Students could examine plants' roles in ecological systems, CO_2 and photosynthesis, how plants use nutrients made available by biological breakdown, how roots create surface areas for substrates and organize nutrient absorption in a substrate matrix, plant competition, and algae.

- *Amphibians:* As with plants, an entire course could be designed around amphibians in vivaria. Subjects of great interest would include: ectothermia, evolution, skin anatomy, limb and tail regeneration, defensive adaptations, reproduction, development, and metamorphosis, as well as ecology and conservation issues.

- *Biosphere science:* Many impassioned vivarists are primarily interested in developing theories and technologies of contained systems analogous to what was attempted but failed in the famous Biosphere 2 experiment in Arizona. The first stage of this area of endeavor is working with open systems such as vivaria using principles of ecological engineering to allow a wide range of species, both plant and animal, to be integrated in culture. Vivarists generally support the keeping and breeding of a wide range of biological organisms in captivity. We want to learn the laws of creating long-lasting, contained ecological systems. Developing systems that could be maintained long-term in space stations for colonization of other planets is another goal of systems vivarists. The ultimate challenge is the design of long-lasting closed systems as was attempted in Biosphere 2. Creating complex vivaria in classrooms is a valuable project that will provide unlimited opportunities for students to work cooperatively and learn about science, biology, ecology, and conservation.

I hold the position that vivaria and aquaria are probably the most important tools that we have for teaching biology and many of the concepts of science. Hopefully, I have shared a glimpse of the endlessly exciting potential of vivaria in education. If you're like me, that simple thought should get your adrenaline rushing and synapses firing.

RECOMMENDED READING

Academy of Sciences. 1996. *Amphibians: Guidelines for the Breeding, Care, and Management of Laboratory Animals.* A Report of the Subcommittee of Amphibian Standards. Academy of Sciences, Washington D.C.

Alcala, A.C. 1986. *Guide to Philippine Flora and Fauna: Amphibians and Reptiles. Vol. 10.* Natural Resources Management Center. Ministry of Natural Resources. University of the Philippines.

Duellman, W. and L. Trueb. 1986. *Biology of Amphibians. John Hopkins University Press. The single most important reference on the subject and a must have for anyone seriously interested in frogs and salamanders.*

Indiviglio, F. 1997. *Newts and Salamanders: A Complete Pet Owner's Manual. Barron's. A valuable reference by an experienced herpetoculturist that also includes husbandry information on species not commonly available in the pet trade.*

Stanicewski, M. 1995. *Amphibians in Captivity. TFH. Highly recommended for anyone with a serious interest in keeping and breeding a variety of salamanders, by one of the few specialists on the subject.*

Wright, K.M. and B.R. Whitaker (eds.). 2001. *Amphibian Medicine and Captive Husbandry.* Krieger Publishing.

Wright, K.M. and D.R. Mader (ed). 1996. *"Amphibian Medicine and Husbandry,"* in *Reptile Medicine and Surgery.* W.B. Saunders.

INDEX

W

water quality, 86, 87
    chlorine, 30
    detecting problems, 30–31
    gas bubble disease, 33–34
    hardness, 32–33
    pH level, 31–32
    purified/distilled water, 32
water changes, 17–18, 28–29, 31, 33, 55, 67, 68
water toads (*Barbourula* spp.), 48
waterdogs (*Ambystoma tigrinum*, larval form), 88–89
wild-caught (WC) specimens, 9, 11
worms (parasites). *See under* diseases/disorders
worms (prey). *See* feeding

ABOUT THE AUTHOR

Philippe de Vosjoli is a highly acclaimed author of the best-selling reptile-care books, The Herpetocultural Library Series. His work in the field of herpetoculture has been recognized nationally and internationally for establishing high standards for amphibian and reptile care. His books, articles, and other writings have been praised and recommended by numerous herpetological societies, veterinarians, and other experts in the field. Philippe de Vosjoli was also the cofounder and president of The American Federation of Herpetoculturists, and was given the Josef Laszlo Memorial Award in 1995 for excellence in herpetoculture and his contribution to the advancement of the field.